ACQUAINTED
WITH AUTISM

God Bless,
Shirli Doany

ACQUAINTED WITH AUTISM

Ministering to Families Affected by Autism

BY SHEILA GOSNEY

Warner Press

Anderson, Indiana

Coordinator of Publishing & Creative Services
Church of God Ministries, Inc.
PO Box 2420, Anderson, IN 46018-2420
800-848-2464 • www.chog.org

To purchase additional copies of this book, to inquire about distribution, and for all other sales-related matters, please contact:

 Warner Press, Inc.
PO Box 2499, Anderson, IN 46018-2499
800-741-7721 • www.warnerpress.org

All Scripture quotations, unless otherwise indicated, are taken from the New King James Version. Copyright © 1982 by Thomas Nelson, Inc. Used by permission. All rights reserved.

Scripture quotations marked NIV are taken from the Holy Bible, New International Version®. NIV®. Copyright © 1973, 1978, 1984 by International Bible Society. Used by permission of Zondervan. All rights reserved.

The information contained in this publication is not intended to serve as a replacement for professional medical advice. Any use of the information in this publication is at the reader's own risk. The author and publisher specifically disclaim any and all liability arising directly or indirectly from the use or application of any information contained herein. A competent health care professional should be consulted regarding your specific situation.

Cover illustration © Shelly Hubel, Southlake, Texas.
Cover design by Mary Jaracz.
Text design by Carolyn Frost.
Edited by Joseph D. Allison and Stephen R. Lewis.
Photos in Chapter 1 and author photo on back cover by Unger Photographic Designs,
    www.ungerphoto.com

ISBN-13: 978-1-59317-494-1

Library of Congress Cataloging-in-Publication Data

Gosney, Sheila.
    Acquainted with autism : ministering to families affected by autism / by Sheila Gosney.
        p.   cm.
    ISBN 978-1-59317-494-1 (pbk.)
    1. Autism in children--Religious aspects--Christianity. 2. Pastoral counseling. I. Title.
    RJ506.A9G675 2009
    618.92'85882--dc22   2009021980

Printed in the United States of America.

09 10 11 12 13 14 15 /VP/ 10 9 8 7 6 5 4 3 2 1

Acquainted with Autism
is dedicated
to all the many families
of children with autism.

May this book offer
compassion and understanding,
renewed courage,
inspiration for ministry,
and, above all, hope in Christ.

May those who read this book realize
the struggles of the many families
affected by autism.

CONTENTS

Acknowledgements . . . . *ix*

Preface . . . . *xi*

Chapter 1: The Beginning of Our Journey 3

Chapter 2: Autism and the Mother 17

Chapter 3: From the Father's Side of the Table 35

Chapter 4: The Siblings' Point of View 49

Chapter 5: Autism's Effect on the Extended Family 61

Chapter 6: Spiritual Encouragement for 69
         Families Affected by Autism

Chapter 7: How Autism Affects Family Finances 79

Chapter 8: How Should the Church Respond to Autism? 89

Chapter 9: Ministering to Families with 109
         Special Circumstances

Chapter 10: Lessons to Learn 115

Afterword 125

Appendix A: The Symptoms and Treatment of Autism 127

Appendix B: Resources 139

To give them beauty for ashes,
The oil of joy for mourning,
The garment of praise for the spirit of heaviness;
That they may be called trees of righteousness,
The planting of the Lord, that He may be glorified.

—Isaiah 61:3b

ACKNOWLEDGEMENTS

This book is not just a book detailing the story of one family, but rather, it's a weaving of individuals whom God placed in our lives and who affected us as we walked this difficult journey.

A simple thank you is not enough to adequately express our gratitude to so many people, but these people are not the kind who have ever sought an eloquent thank you for their support to our family.

To our family on both sides, the Gosney and Hammock families, thank you for the outpouring of love, support, and shared tears in our struggles with Taylor. It is quite wonderful to also share tears of joy with you as we reflect on how far God has brought us.

Thank you to every school teacher who showed kindness to our son as you worked with him. Your service to Taylor will never be forgotten.

Thank you to every aide who went home weary after school but woke up the next day to greet Taylor at school.

Thank you to the doctors, therapists, and nurses who touched our son's life. May God bless you and may you know that Jehovah Rapha used you on Taylor's behalf.

Many thanks to all our brothers and sisters in Christ who continually lifted us in prayer through the most difficult years and still today as we continue living with autism.

Many thanks to Mary, who has cut Taylor's hair for years. If not for your patience, Taylor would have never had a haircut.

Thanks always to the Lorenson family, who opened their home and hearts, letting Taylor come over so we could have a break.

Thank you to every person who looked past our son's disability to see a beautiful child of great value and potential.

Thank you to everyone who expressed compassion to us on our most difficult days, for it was seen and recorded in our hearts.

Finally, all praise, honor, and glory goes to our Lord Jesus Christ, who takes ashes of sorrow and turns them into beauty for His glory.

Who has believed our report?
And to whom has the arm of the LORD been revealed?
For He shall grow up before Him as a tender plant,
And as a root out of dry ground.
He has no form or comeliness;
And when we see Him,
There is no beauty that we should desire Him.
He is despised and rejected by men,
A Man of sorrows and acquainted with grief.
And we hid, as it were, our faces from Him;
He was despised, and we did not esteem Him.
Surely He has borne our griefs
And carried our sorrows;
Yet we esteemed Him stricken,
Smitten by God, and afflicted.
But He was wounded for our transgressions,
He was bruised for our iniquities;
The chastisement for our peace was upon Him,
And by His stripes we are healed

—Isaiah 53:1–5

PREFACE

Chances are, if you picked this book up, you already know someone with autism. It could be a relative, neighbor, co-worker's child, or a family in your church who has an autistic child. While hardly any adults today grew up knowing someone with autism, hardly any of us can now say we haven't seen someone touched by this disorder. Today, the issue of autism hits far too close to home, often landing in our own circle of family and friends. Autism is becoming far too personal to this generation.

The statistics of this disorder are staggering. As of the writing of this book, the rate of new diagnoses is 1 in 150 births in the United States, and similar statistics are being recorded in other countries. That is startling to say the least. It's a disorder that remains a mystery to some degree, and the mounting numbers only add to the mystery.

The purpose of this book is to glorify God by giving you a glimpse into the personal lives of families who have autistic children and by teaching you how to minister to them. In this book, I share the intimate daily life of my own family with you in order to reveal what life with autism is really like. But I also share thoughts and opinions of other families to show you the common ground we share in this journey. Here are some comments I've heard over the years from parents of autistic children. As you read this book, perhaps these will shed light on the feelings and emotions we all carry:

"I just wish people had a clue what my life is really like."

"I wish people knew how exhausted I am every day."

"I wish that when I tell people I cannot do something, they would believe me."

"I want people to know my autistic child has feelings and understands things they don't believe he does."

"I'd like to tell people with normal kids to stop taking things for granted and stop complaining so much."

"Sometimes I just feel so lonely."

"I feel like I am living a surreal world where everything is about autism from morning to night. I struggle to make conversation with people about everyday things."

Remember as you read this account that our stories are quite similar. The names change, but we all share the same emotions. If you have ever wondered what it is like to raise an autistic child, you will wonder no more after reading this book. Here, our family becomes an open book, and I hope that you will see the faith in God that has carried us all these years. God is truly the most important part of our story, and we give all glory to Him for any benefit our testimony brings.

God, in his sovereignty, allowed my family to enter into this experience called autism. I now believe his purpose was to enable me to write this book. Over the years, many sincere Christians have approached me—often with tears in their eyes—asking what they could do to help. I believe most people have no idea what they can do, mainly because the disorder is so foreign to them. In this book, I will describe very specific ways you can minister to exhausted families like ours. As you finish each individual chapter, it will flow right into ministry ideas pertaining to the theme of that chapter. Many of the acts of kindness described in this book have been done for my family, some have been related to me by other families, and others reflect the unmet needs described by parents of autistic children. While reading these ideas, remember that the Holy Spirit is able to guide you to your own ministry for the families you know. (The most exciting chapter is likely the one that explains how churches can create specialized ministries for the inclusion of children with autism, thus welcoming the entire family.)

Because autism is a complex disorder, this book also features an appendix that describes its various symptoms and characteristics. Each symptom is detailed in Appendix A in very readable terms that laypersons can easily understand. It is certainly not an exhaustive description, but it includes the basic knowledge to get you started. Many of your questions about autism will be answered in this chapter. You may read this chapter first, or stop and read it at any point in the book at which you feel the need to educate yourself on the disorder. Use the information as a springboard to help you build relationships with families of autistic children and ask further questions of them.

While this book does not debate the various theories about the causes of autism, you will read of the treatment that helped our son the most. It was our answer to prayer, so I could not omit it. Perhaps it will aid in the healing of another child. The primary goal of this book remains to teach you what autism really means for a family and to guide you to effectively minister to them.

Scripture describes Jesus as "a Man of Sorrows, acquainted with grief." Jesus never distanced Himself from pain but rather walked right up to it and dissolved any misconceptions that there were in the moment. Although Jesus is the true Healer, He often uses us to minister to those around us who are suffering. It's my belief that the body of Christ is eager to know how to minister to families suffering with autism. Christians simply need to be educated and enlightened about this disorder. While no one can do it all, this book will cause you to realize there is something everyone can do to help. It uncovers a goldmine of opportunity for ministry to these hurting families. Let's remove the mystery together and cover autism with the love of Christ.

Sheila Gosney

This I recall to my mind,
Therefore I have hope.
Through the LORD's mercies we are not consumed,
Because His compassions fail not.
They are new every morning;
Great is Your faithfulness.
"The LORD is my portion," says my soul,
"Therefore I hope in Him!"

—*Lamentations 3:21-24* NKJV

FAITH FOUND A GARDEN

I've learned a few things in the course of hardship
that are priceless, steadfast and true.

I've learned no matter how hard this life gets
the Lord won't forget about you.

I've learned that at times your spirit gets tired
and your faith can get low and depleted.

But the faithfulness of God never gets exhausted
and comes in to supply what is needed.

I've learned you can live through enormous crisis
that doesn't seem to have reason or rhyme.

But somehow and some way God turns them to riches
through His wisdom and passage of time.

I've learned that the deficits & shortages of life
were not meant to cause heartache or shame.

For they made me look up to God's well of provision
and trust in the strength of His name.

I've learned it's the hard times that teach us the most
about God and His character of old.

For it's during those seasons I clung to His Word
and every promise that He's ever told.

I've been refined in my heart and my mind
because He tendered me through difficult years.

And faith found a garden in the soil of my heart
that was watered by all of my tears.

CHAPTER 1

The Beginning of Our Journey

Have you ever started watching a movie in which you really liked the main characters but the story line became traumatic and difficult to watch? By the middle of the show, you found yourself begging for the story to end on a better note. This is the way our family, friends, and church felt as the diagnosis of autism was made for our son Taylor and during the subsequent difficult years when things escalated beyond our control.

Most parents of autistic children can easily tell you the day their world started changing. For some, it was the day of diagnosis. For others, it was the day they began to realize that something was not right with their child's development. Our story began in October 1995, around our son Taylor's first birthday. Taylor's first year of life was basically normal, except that he passed a few milestones a little later than our previous two sons. Just prior to his first birthday, Taylor had made the first sounds of normal speech. He looked right at me and said, "Mama." Soon, he began to look at my husband and say, "Dada." We were amused that he would look right at us after being asked a question and grin while shaking his head, saying, "No, No, No." We seemed to be seeing a little personality developing, just like most parents see at about that age.

However, things quickly started falling apart. By the week following that first birthday, I realized I wasn't hearing Taylor say my name anymore. As a matter of fact, I heard none of the words he had already mastered. I started paying close attention, listening for the words, even giving Taylor the opportunity to say them. I got right up in his darling face and said, "Say 'Mama,' Taylor. Just say, 'Mama.'" But no matter how much I begged or prodded, all I heard was silence. Where words had once been, there was now empty silence.

Not long after that, the silence was replaced with strange noises, repetitive syllables, and unusual body movements. Some days I heard, "Dugga-dugga-dugga," the entire day.

Taylor began laughing for hours on end and then later prancing around the house on tiptoes instead of walking normally. His interest in toys shifted dramatically. He had a normal interest in toys prior to his first birthday, but now he didn't play with them. Instead, he tore parts from the toys and carried the parts around for long periods of time. He began flipping toy cars over and spinning the wheels as fast as he could. Hyperactivity dramatically increased; suddenly I had a toddler who was more active but yet didn't speak anymore. He exhibited behaviors I had never seen in my life. Early signs of Obsessive Compulsive Disorder were being manifested. Taylor would do strange things, such as carrying around a grocery-store receipt for days until it fell apart. Nobody could touch the current item of his obsession, and it wasn't pleasant when Taylor couldn't locate it.

In the months that rolled between his first and second birthdays, Taylor was constantly changing, adding one new symptom after another. *Who is this child and where did my Taylor go?* I asked myself constantly, but no answer was forthcoming.

Sleeplessness became a huge problem for Taylor. He was not napping during the day or sleeping at night. He often went to bed as late as midnight and got up around 4:00 a.m. If he ever slept until daybreak, I considered it a miracle. Naps during the day were rare and seemed to make him sleep even less at night. I simply dragged myself around the house in a stupor, wondering what could be the problem and what anyone could do to help. He never seemed tired from his all-night episodes, but I was exhausted.

Not long after the sleeplessness began, hypersensory problems became part of the package. Taylor was easily overstimulated visually and disturbed emotionally. Soon, I had a child I wanted to avoid taking anywhere. Going out in public was more than I could handle and clearly more than he could handle. When we entered a store, signs that hung from the ceiling advertising the weekly sales made him scream until we just had to leave, sometimes abandoning our groceries in the cart. It took several trips to the store to discover exactly what triggered his hysterical reactions. (I watched his eyes and finally figured it out.) It got so bad that I had to arrange for a sitter or take Taylor and his brothers to their grandparents when I needed to make a trip to a store. Every move we made outside the home now required meticulous plotting, planning, and scheduling. Even then, we had to cancel many appointments at a moment's notice because we were having an unusually bad day. I felt that if we were barely coping at home, the situation would only worsen in public, and I was right.

Taylor had an excellent ability to make eye contact his first year of life, and he maintained this ability during the second year of life, although many other problems were being manifested. While most autistics have poor eye contact, he seemed to struggle with this issue only on occasion. However, Taylor did develop a strange aversion to seeing his own reflection in a mirror or other shiny surfaces. When we took him to our bathroom mirror and held him up to

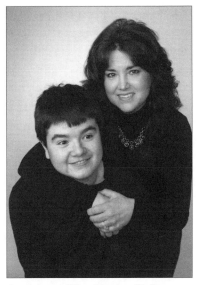

Our Journey of Hope Together. **Sheila Gosney and her youngest son, Taylor Gosney.**

see himself, he would dart his eyes everywhere around the mirror to avoid looking at his own face. We would tap the mirror in an attempt to get him to look at himself, but to no avail. Many times I wondered what was going on in that pretty little head and what pain it caused him to see himself. Only God knows what suffering goes on in the bodies of those afflicted with this disorder.

When Taylor was around eighteen months of age, I expressed concern to a pediatrician about his odd behaviors and delayed development. He examined him and reassured me that he didn't believe it was anything serious; he certainly didn't believe it was autism. I told the doctor that Taylor no longer looked toward me when his name was spoken. Even if I called his name loudly from a short distance away, he would sit with eyes glazed, unmoving. The doctor agreed we should test his hearing, the first of many tests to be done over the years. It was determined that Taylor's hearing was just fine. The doctor's staff could offer no new pieces for the puzzle, other than the knowledge that Taylor was not deaf.

The pediatrician told me to go home, wait it out, and try not to worry. A big part of me really wanted to believe him. Who wants to live with constant worry and nagging fear? But I also knew I had a child with problems that no one could explain to me thus far. I had two older sons, so I felt like I was a pro at raising boys by this point. But I had never experienced anything like this in my years of being a mother. Taylor left me scratching my head. Anxiety was a part of every hour of the day. Every strange symptom created a new question in my mind.

Time seemed to crawl between that pediatrician's visit and Taylor's second birthday. Every day was another day of waiting to see if the problems would go away, another day of praying that they would, but they didn't. Each new symptom only confirmed the suspicion that we were looking at a serious problem. Just prior to Taylor's second birthday, we made a trip to an autism clinic in Columbia, Missouri, where a specialist gave Taylor the diagnosis of autism. It was a shock on some level, but on another level it was not. God has a way of preparing us for some things, and my own mother was the one God used to prepare me for this news. Despite the pediatrician's insistence that Taylor was just slow to develop, my mother kept saying that she knew it was more than that. She insisted the pediatrician was wrong. She talked with a friend who had dealt with autism and described Taylor's behaviors to her. That friend felt Taylor had autism and told me so.

I also had a dear friend named Donna Long whose son Luke had been diagnosed with autism the previous year. One day, I called and told her of my mother's concerns. She came right over with a large notebook full of autism information for me to read. She watched Taylor in my living room for a while and said, "Oh, my." Then she left the notebook for me to mull over. (I heard her saying, "Oh, my," in my head for hours after she left.) I cried my heart out on the pages of her notebook. Every symptom of Taylor's that had puzzled me was mentioned in the medical articles in Donna's binder. One article after another pointed to the truth before my eyes. It was almost as if I was reading a story of Taylor's life thus far. All the bizarre symptoms and behaviors had a name, and it was *autism*.

Not all parents get a head start on the knowledge of such a diagnosis, but for some reason God graced me with a clue before the official diagnosis. On the day the doctor spoke that word to me, I had already made peace with the idea. It was almost a relief to hear it in definitive terms, tearing the shroud of mystery. Even the doctor said she had never seen such a calm reaction when she delivered the diagnosis of autism to a parent. She had no idea I'd already cried in private. Plenty more tears would fall as the years progressed and we struggled for answers in Taylor's treatment. I had to learn to balance the tears with my own well-being. There were some days I felt like crying so badly but was afraid to start. I feared that if I started, I might not stop crying, that I would lose my mind from the stress, that I would waste precious energy that I needed to keep going. I knew I had to control the tears, but they were always right under the surface, ever present.

Suddenly, the task of raising three young boys had turned into a life we'd never dreamed of, practically overnight. The days dissolved into a sea of doctor's appointments, in-home visits from professionals, and books to read on the subject of autism. I was often overwhelmed. I had to learn how to live day by day, sometimes hour by hour. Taylor was assigned a caseworker from the DMH (Department of Mental Health), a wonderful lady by the name of Monica King. On one of Monica's first visits, we filled out paperwork and chatted, I looked at her at one point and asked, "So I am going to be a special-needs mother now?" She seemed a bit surprised by the question, but she smiled back tenderly and said yes, that was indeed what I was going to be. At that point, I had no clue that we were actually becoming a special-needs household, that autism would affect every member of our family in different ways. Our ordeal was just getting started.

Some symptoms left us baffled and heartbroken. But as autism began robbing our son of normalcy, he also began doing things we found very intriguing. Taylor started showing signs of high intelligence after his first birthday. He exhibited a very strong interest in anything written and loved seeing words. He was drawn to any television show with writing on the screen. The evening newscast became his preference because stock-market quotes scrolled across the TV at the end of the show. Taylor wobbled in as soon as he heard the news coming on and sat riveted until the stock market statistics appeared, and then he became very happy and excited. He also loved watching the credits roll at the end of any of his videos. Most kids wander off during the credits, but not Taylor. They were the best part of the show for him. At one point, he even learned how to rewind a videotape to just the right point so he could watch the credits all over again.

Taylor also became fascinated with any written material around the house. Anything with writing on it had to be right-side up at all times. Magazines laying on the living room floor would get kicked around in all dif-

A Night of Answered Prayer. **Taylor winks at the photographer during a break at Terry's wedding.**

ferent directions. Taylor would come over immediately if he saw this, turn them right-side up, and then walk away contented. At first, I reasoned that he couldn't possibly recognize the letters. How could a child do this if he hadn't been taught the alphabet? He was far too young. He was a toddler. But if he didn't know the alphabet, how did he know that the letters were upside-down?

I decided to test him myself. I got out the children's wooden alphabet blocks and lined them up on the windowsill of my living room, where the boys all played with their cars. They were just at eye level. I got out every block in the set and lined them up, flipping about 20 percent of them upside-down, leaving the rest right-side up. Then I sat back and waited. I will never forget what happened next. Taylor bounded into the room as most toddlers do, with a bouncy jaunt. Suddenly, he froze in his tracks, whipping his head around to the window. Going over, he immediately flipped all the upside-down blocks until they were right-side up and then wandered back out of the room. I sat with my jaw hanging open.

Later, we spoke to a pediatric neurologist who, like us, has a son with autism, telling him of Taylor's unusual ability with letters. He told us that his own son's gift for reading had became evident at a young age. He assured us that Taylor was reading already, that what he had done with the alphabet blocks proved it. He told us that Taylor was likely of high intelligence. In the years that followed, when things went so terribly bad, I clung to the memory of that conversation. I had to believe that Taylor—the real Taylor—was alive and well underneath the autism. And he was.

Taylor's disorder continued to manifest itself in the years that followed. At age three, we enrolled him in the Early Childhood Special Education Pre-School, which was part of our Monroe City public school system. It was a struggle for Taylor, but the staff there worked hard, striving to get him farther along than he was. There were occasional victories, but Taylor's persistent problems with autism often overshadowed any progress made. While they had encountered autism before, they had never had a case quite as complex as Taylor's.

We continued in the special education program of the public school system until Taylor started the first grade. Taylor attended school with the benefit of his own aide, Donetta Murray. She never left his side and proved to be a valuable person in our lives. Everyone at school wanted so badly for Taylor to have a better life, but the autism continued to escalate. His sensitivity to sensory overstimulation increased, and he clearly needed a setting that the public school could not provide. Taylor also began to make very loud noises, greatly hindering his ability to stay mainstreamed in a regular classroom setting. We knew that the other students could not learn to their fullest ability with Taylor's noises in their ears all day. At this point, Taylor also entered a phase of aggressiveness. Since he could not communicate verbally, he became upset when he couldn't tell people what was bothering him or what he wanted. The older Taylor got, the more he knew what he wanted and the more agitated he became when he couldn't tell us about it. Sometimes, it was something as simple as a florescent light fixture making a low buzzing noise, which sounded like a motorcycle engine to him. If a teacher rearranged the schedule for the day, that could set him off. I couldn't imagine having needs and desires that I could not communicate to others. Taylor acted out his frustrations in the only way he could, and it wasn't a good situation. Taylor had become the proverbial square peg in a round hole. His needs increased to the point that a change was clearly in order.

We marked a turning point in Taylor's life when we had him tested for the Mississippi Valley State School in nearby Hannibal, Missouri. This school is strictly for individuals with severe disabilities, enrolling only students who pass stringent state tests. Taylor met the requirements and was enrolled in the fall of 2001 as he was turning seven years old. To be honest, I had always feared that Taylor would have to enter a state school. I wanted to hang onto his mainstreamed status. But my fears proved to be unfounded. The state school has been a wonderful resource for Taylor. It provides him with an education on a daily basis full of academic learning and helps him grow both socially and physically. He gets all the therapies he needs on a daily basis as part of the schooling. If he has a bad day, his therapies can be adjusted. Everything at this school is geared to the individual student's abilities, and students are challenged to keep progressing each day. The blessings that God has given us through this school cannot be adequately described. I've often said there is no separation of church and state because my heavenly Father passes through any wall where my children go. When Taylor's bus comes home each afternoon, he comes back more balanced. I get the break that I desperately need because he is with professionals who also care about him.

When Taylor was about eight and a half, his autism went totally haywire. He had always had some level of OCD (obsessive-compulsive disorder), even from the earliest days of his autism symptoms. But it was always a manageable problem and was even cute at times. At the onset, Taylor might carry around as many golf balls as his little hands could clutch. Or he might watch the same video all day long for weeks on end. But then the OCD became so acute that our family nearly gave up. Taylor became visually obsessed with dust and dirt particles, and he wanted to look at them on the floor or along baseboards of any room he entered. He got so aggressive at times that he would toss furniture out of his way and break things, just to get to the baseboard. He peeled the rubber baseboards off his classroom at school during this time, thinking there might be dust behind them that he could see.

Even in public, Taylor might drop to his knees and hunt for dust. I held back the tears when he did this and people stared. They would look at Taylor on all fours and then look up to me, as if I could stop him or offer an explanation for what he was doing. I had no explanation because even I didn't know why he craved such a thing.

Taylor also developed an obsession with cracks and crevices. He began to pour liquids along cracks to see what would happen. Everyone in our house and at school tried desperately to keep liquids out of sight, but it was too difficult. He would get his hands on anything, liquid detergents and hand soaps, for example, and pour them along the crack where the carpet met the baseboard so he could watch the liquid ooze along the crack. He stood there and made peculiar noises, flapping his hands as the liquids made their way along the crack. We still have liquid detergent stains along the walls of our living room, red cough syrup on one wall, and stains from an entire bottle of bubble bath in another room. They are visual reminders of a very painful chapter in our lives.

Of all the phases of Taylor's life, this was by far the most disturbing for everyone involved. Nobody knew what to do with a boy who crawled around on all fours, doing such abnormal things. We had no clue why this obsession had suddenly descended to this level. We nearly placed Taylor in a long-term care facility because we were so exhausted. It was especially draining for me as his mother. I was continually on edge, trying to keep Taylor from damaging things or hurting himself. We drove out to look at the facility; both my husband and I cried the entire way home. After a few days of reflection, we decided we just couldn't do it. We had no idea how we would continue to care for Taylor, his behavior having become as destructive as it was, but we both felt we might have a nervous breakdown if we placed Taylor in an institution. He was our child, and we hung on for dear life, desperate to find another way.

We had no energy left for elaborate prayers. Our prayers became simple pleas for an answer.

The clinic that treated Taylor's autism offered us drugs when we first reported this dramatic change in his behavior. We gave them to Taylor in desperation. We tried one drug after another in an effort to modify this behavior, but things only got worse. The medications would dull his erratic behavior for a short time, but then even more bizarre side effects kicked in. One drug created a huge appetite, and Taylor craved sugar all hours of the day, causing him to gain an alarming amount of weight in a short time. One night, in the middle of the might, I heard noises and thought we might have had a break-in. But when we investigated, we found Taylor sitting on the kitchen counter eating sugar right out of the canister with his hands cupped to his mouth. We dropped that drug and moved on to another. At one point, Taylor developed a potentially life-altering disorder called tardive dyskinesia caused by the medications he was using. The disorder caused involuntary muscle movements and restricted his breathing by attacking the lungs. Taylor would desperately stretch out his neck and

11

gasp for breath. There wasn't a thing we could do except stand by him and talk to him, waiting for the episode to pass.

We had never prayed so hard in our whole lives as we did during this time. We stopped giving Taylor the drugs, but we knew from the medical articles we had read that tardive dyskinesia does not always disappear. Once it starts, it is often a permanent affliction. Our hearts simply could not bear the idea that a boy with autism, unable to communicate with us, would also have attacks that robbed him of the ability to breathe. Each day after Taylor left for school, I laid face down on the floor, begging the Lord to reverse it. My poor husband had to pull himself together enough to do his job. He worked and prayed at the same time. At least I was able to fall apart behind closed doors. My tears became prayers, and my prayers became tears.

During this harrowing ordeal, many Christian friends supported us with prayer. I think that was the longest two weeks of our lives, waiting to see whether the disorder would pass. After about ten days, the symptoms began diminishing. Then Taylor stopped jerking around and his breathing returned to normal. I will always remember this as one of the most dramatic and remarkable answers to prayer on Taylor's behalf. Even now, if I see the words *tardive dyskinesia* in print, I gasp, recalling our horrific ordeal.

The episode with tardive dyskinesia made us realize it was time for a whole new approach. We were facing a decisive fork in the road. As Taylor's parents, our impression was that the medications were not helping his condition or relieving the most troublesome symptoms. We began weaning Taylor off all of his medications with the doctor's assistance. I also began reading a book on treating autism with natural substances instead of drugs. The whole concept was new to me, and I was intrigued by every page. The book contained story after story of clinics where medical doctors treated autism with natural substances. It also shared the children's stories of improvement. Some had recovered from the autism so much so that onlookers could barely discern them from their normal peers.

As I read each chapter, I told my husband all about it. We became convinced this was what we should try next for Taylor. We chose a clinic described in the book, the Pfeiffer Treatment Center in Warrenville, Illinois.

In the months between the removal of the medications and our trip to the clinic, I tried some natural supplements on my own and saw noticeable improvements in Taylor. They were the first glimmers of hope we had seen in years; although they were small, they were a delight to see. We purposely did not tell many people that we were trying the natural supplement at home because we didn't want hopeful people to be looking for improvement; we wanted them to see Taylor with unbiased eyes. Our quiet approach worked; other people did start noticing the improvement in Taylor's behaviors and commented on them, including the staff at his school. We felt we were on the right track and could hardly wait to get to the new clinic and have Taylor evaluated.

On our first visit to Pfeiffer Treatment Center, Taylor underwent blood tests and urine tests, as well as having a hair sample removed for testing. The staff carefully evaluated Taylor's metabolic condition. We learned a great deal on that visit. We learned even more a few weeks later when Taylor's lab reports came in. We realized that autism isn't "just autism" but that the body's chemistry plays a significant role in the cause and effect. We learned that some aspects of autism can be treated by

My Three Sons. **Terry Pettitt, 25 (left), Tyler Gosney, 15 (right), Taylor Gosney, 14, (foreground).**

changing an individual's diet and environment. Heavy metal toxicities are often a factor with autism, and Taylor had abnormal levels of several heavy metals in his body. We learned that Taylor's gastrointestinal tract was not working properly. Taylor also had recurring yeast infections. The center gave us a game plan for treating them and explained why it was so crucial. We even learned the name of the metabolic disorder that was largely responsible for the OCD that had nearly destroyed our family's life. The lab reports helped the doctors at Pfeiffer Treatment Center identify the metabolic problems inside his body and determine which nutrients and natural substances would best help Taylor. They developed a personalized supplement plan for us to use in Taylor's treatment. Every metabolic disturbance was explained in detail, and we were educated on why each one created the symptoms that it did. We felt we had discovered something very big. Puzzle pieces were falling into place that had been missing for years.

Taylor's new daily plan was set. I would administer natural supplements to him instead of drugs. I prayed over the bottles as they arrived and asked God to have his way with Taylor by using them for healing. Surprisingly, Taylor took the supplements with very little resistance. Even to this day, I rarely have much trouble with Taylor taking what I bring him. Occasionally, he fights me and I tell him that I know he's happier now and that the supplements help him stay that way. He seems to know what I mean, because he stops fighting me and takes the supplement cup. Some people who see him take his supplements consider it a miracle, but we know God still works miracles.

The changes in Taylor were quite dramatic. Within months, we saw evidence that the supplements were helping Taylor. Some started jokingly referring to Taylor as the poster child for the natural treatment of autism. It was hard not to agree with them, considering the transformation that we saw taking place right before our eyes.

We had high hopes that Taylor would start talking after the treatments because many nonverbal children with autism do. But we're still waiting

The Gosney Family. Front row (l. to r.:) Stephanie Pettitt and Bret Gosney; back row (l. to r.:) Terry Pettitt, Tyler Gosney, Sheila Gosney, and Taylor Gosney.

for that miracle. We hold out hope that we will still see it someday. Until then, we are grateful for the progress we have enjoyed. Even though he has limited speech abilities, he has found new ways to communicate what he wants. For example, he has begun writing down words when he wants to communicate. The first few times Taylor did this, we carried the papers with us to show everybody we met—it was that exciting! We believe cylinders in his mind are now clicking that could unlock the door to better health. Definitely, healing has come to Taylor's system.

Taylor does things at school that amaze us. The reports are staggering at times and remind us of how far we've come. Taylor does math, plays on a computer, and has developed a sense of humor. He is a far more teachable and trainable young man than ever before. He is also able to conduct himself better in social settings.

Is he still autistic? Yes, he is. But he is clearly not the child he was when he was crawling around obsessed with dirt. Most people who see Taylor infrequently express amazement at how much he's progressed since they last saw him. Currently, Taylor is stepping into puberty, and we have to adjust his supplements more carefully than before. The ever-changing hormones of puberty disrupt his body chemistry. Battling yeast continues to be very important. But we have learned to modify Taylor's plan when these problems arise. We just have to make adjustments patiently until we find the right balance. Taylor takes three or four rounds of supplements every day and probably will do so for the rest of his life.

I enjoy telling this part of our story because it's the most exciting thing we've experienced in our years of heartache with autism. Our fork in the road led us to what we needed all along. We endured many years when things only got worse, but it is refreshing to be able to tell a story of encouragement. God hears the prayers of his people, and in his perfect timing, he answers them as he sees fit. I believe this was the outcome that our friends longed to see during all those years of heartache. They never knew quite what they were praying for, but God did.

As you can tell, my family is convinced that the natural treatment of autism helps the most. Drugs may not be wrong for some physical disorders, but I truly believe nutritional supplements are more healing for this disorder. Nutrient therapy helps everything else the child with autism receives (e.g., occupational therapy, school training) to work together better. If you are reading this and would like to know more about this approach,

I encourage you to visit the Pfeiffer Treatment Center's Web site for more information (see appendix 2) or to find a DAN! doctor. DAN! means "Defeat Autism Now!", and these doctors use the same type of approaches as I have described in our story. There are many DAN! doctors in the United States; a quick search of the Internet will reveal listings of DAN! doctors in many states.

This chapter only gives you a timeline of our lives thus far. I have much to tell you in the pages ahead, where you will get to know our family in a personal way. But I hope this book encourages you to become personally acquainted with the families of children with autism. Every child on the planet is unique, and each child with autism is unique as well. If you are to learn how to minister to them effectively, you must get to know them personally.

> *My frame was not hidden from You,*
> *When I was made in secret,*
> *And skillfully wrought in the lowest parts of the earth.*
> *Your eyes saw my substance, being yet unformed.*
> *And in Your book they all were written,*
> *The days fashioned for me,*
> *When as yet there were none of them.*
> —Psalm 139:15–16

CHAPTER 2

Autism and the Mother

N o situation in my life has changed me as much as being the mother of a child with autism. On a spiritual level, I would also say this unique role has taught me more about what it truly means to walk in dependence upon the Lord. Nearly everything about life changes after autism enters your world. It is as if one day the Lord reaches down from heaven and hands you a new pair of glasses and you have to look at everything through the lens of autism. Every decision you make in your life from that point on is determined according to the autism of your child. You are no longer just a wife and mother; you are now a woman in charge of figuring out what to do for the betterment of a child with a major disability. You are literally a mother with a mission.

Having to cope with having a child with autism breaks you at the same time that it humbles you. There's a certain amount of grief and heartache you must continually learn to process and give back to God. Over the years, many have asked me how I have dealt with it. It's a hard question to answer quickly, because it has many aspects, but ultimately it all comes down to God and his grace. The anguish of having a child who appears normal at birth and who develops but then regresses is almost indescribable. We had two older sons, Terry and Tyler, and this was nothing like we had encountered with them.

Taylor's baby book is nearly empty. There are a few notations and dates in it up to the point that the autism started manifesting itself. I had never had a child who manifested normal childhood development and then reverted before my eyes. How does a mother fill in a date for an accomplishment that then disappears? Does she also write in the date that it disappeared? A mystery was unfolding before our eyes, so I found it easier to stop writing in the book. When the regression began, the baby book was shoved into a kitchen cabinet because the book itself was a reminder that things were not right in my son's world. I've opened it a few times over the years and had to shut it because the pain is as fresh as it was when the autism first hit. Some pain gets better with time, but a certain amount of motherly pain is just always there, ready to trigger a fresh tear.

I am not sure I could fully describe what a diagnosis of autism does to a mother's emotions. Each woman digests the diagnosis in different ways. Some are racked with false guilt and try to figure out if they did something to cause it. Doctors and common sense tell you that's not true, but nagging doubts haunt you in quiet moments when you least expect them. I struggled at times with these thoughts. I had been unable to take prenatal vitamins during my pregnancy with Taylor, so I often wondered if the autism was caused by this. It took time and much prayer to overcome that idea.

Mothers are supposed to know their babies intimately, yet I was almost strangled with my questions of what was going on and why. The onset of Taylor's disorder made me feel like we were stuck in a dark tunnel, wondering when someone would find and rescue us. We could hear the footsteps of the doctors on the ground above us. We could hear all the "normal" people in the outside world. My spirit just cried for someone to come and yank me and my baby out of the pit. I suspected something was seriously wrong, and I needed a name for it. And yet when I heard that name, it brought a life-altering diagnosis with it.

Not long after Taylor's diagnosis, I told a local woman what we had learned. She listened for a bit and then asked me, "What will you do if he gets worse?" I was taken aback by the question and told her that I didn't think he would get worse. But that is exactly what would unfold as the early years progressed. There have been seasons of this journey when I was certain I would break emotionally, but, praise God, I did not. The early years were the roughest by far. There were days on end when Taylor would sleep little during the day and be incredibly active during the night. Many times, my husband would stay up for a shift during the night, but I seemed to fare the worst after these long spells with no sleep.

At the time of Taylor's diagnosis, I also began developing abnormal physical symptoms of my own. It turned out that I had auto-immune problems, which the stress of dealing with autism aggravated. I battled my own aching body while my heart broke in two. One problem seemed to compete with the other for my attention. My doctor told me to avoid stress and get some rest, but I had a child who ran my legs off every day. I confess that at times I questioned God and wondered how much I could take, but that mental state only stifled my faith, so I didn't let myself stay there long. I knew I had work to do and I needed my faith to keep going.

Evening and morning and at noon,
I will pray, and cry aloud,
And He shall hear my voice.
—Psalm 55:17

Many autistic children are nonverbal, including Taylor. From his youngest days, he knew exactly what he wanted; I could tell by the way he acted that he was trying to express a very specific thought. He just had no words to express himself and could not figure out other methods to communicate with us. Over a period of many years, Taylor could only throw himself on the floor, kicking, screaming, and pushing us around in an effort to relay what was bothering him. Sometimes I could guess what he wanted, but the most desperate times were when I had no clue whatsoever and the screaming would go on for long stretches of time. People would often ask me what he wanted. With tears in my eyes, I could only reply, "I don't know! I just don't know!"

The mother of a child with autism tends to question herself quite a bit each day, always wondering if she's doing the right thing and if there's something else she needs to educate herself on. I was no exception. Those first few years brought so much learning for me as a mother and also for my family. At times it seemed we had been dropped off in a foreign country where we didn't know the language and had to learn how to communicate and figure things out.

I soon realized that Taylor had no sense of boundaries or danger. Most small children need to be watched, but I had to watch him like a hawk at all times, even as he moved from room to room in our own house. I couldn't trust him to be alone in his room because of what he might do to himself.

Once when I did one of my checks on his whereabouts, I discovered him in his room holding a butter knife about an inch from sticking it into an electrical socket. These frequent incidents only heightened the anxiety I felt and the amount of checking I felt I had to do. Taylor couldn't wander around our yard without someone watching his every move. He would either walk out in the street or simply wander away. My neighbors have seen me "on patrol" at every hour of the day, creeping around bushes and trees to watch Taylor from a distance and call out when he was going too far. To this day, I must continue to patrol Taylor's whereabouts. Although he is older and doing better, he is still prone to wandering away. I call these Taylor's "private field trips." I am the chaperone who follows from a distance.

As their mother and main caregiver, I felt utterly overwhelmed being at home all day with the boys, trying to figure out from hour to hour what to do to with Taylor. The sheer responsibility made me dread the hours my husband was gone. It truly was a moment-by-moment existence. Some days I felt stronger, but most days I melted from the physical stress and fatigue. I recall crouching down in my kitchen on the floor and sitting with my back against the kitchen cabinets, just to take a mental break from the stress. I felt so low and emotionally worn out that sitting on the floor made sense. But I knew that eventually I had to get up. Someone on the other side of the counter always needed me.

Although I had struggled with periods of loneliness, I had no idea that autism would bring a sense of loneliness to the entire family. Because we could not take Taylor to many public places, we remained at home quite a bit, especially during his early years. Play dates with other mothers were nearly impossible and were often cancelled moments before we were due at their houses. It seemed as if our life consisted of going to medical and therapy appointments and just staying at home. I remember standing at my front window staring out at the cars driving up and down my street. I had been in one of those cars once, able to come and go as I pleased; but now I was confined to the house. Sometimes I looked at people walking by our house and wondered what they would do or say if they had a clue about what strange lives we lived behind closed doors. I knew most people would never believe it; I was still trying to believe it myself. There we were—on an island, only fifteen feet from the street. Yet on that lonely island God spoke to me. I learned that he could be faithful in the most desperate circumstances, and I came to discover how beautiful his voice sounded. I became so dependent upon God after Taylor's diagnosis of autism that he literally became my everything. He was the one I turned to, the one who knew everything that was happening to us. I never had to convince God how strange and bizarre our lives were; he was there and he knew.

For in the time of trouble
He shall hide me in His pavilion;
In the secret place of His tabernacle
He shall hide me;
He shall set me high upon a rock.
—Psalm 27:5

The mother of a child with autism realizes early on that challenges lie ahead of her. And if she has other children, she has even more to balance on a daily basis. Who would get my attention at each moment? Who needs me the most? It's a frenzy which only the Father of Peace can calm.

Many people saw my focus on Taylor, who had many problems, but I was always worried for my other sons. I wondered how living with so much abnormality was going to affect them. Sometimes I looked at my other two boys and thought they only had a shell of a mother because so much of me was spent on their brother. The early years were so stressful that I believe the stress has blocked some of our memory of those years. We struggle to recall things that a family should be able to recall. Even now, my husband and I look at old photos of our other two sons and honestly can't remember them at that age.

In that desperation and stress, I learned to give God what bothered me the most. I accepted the fact that our lives weren't normal anymore, and I knew we couldn't change it, so I learned to pray on a different level. Prayer became more frequent but far more personal and intense. I learned that prayer is heard less for its eloquence and more for the dependence of the soul who prays. I learned to walk and pray at the same time, often while trying to keep up with my kids. Sometimes prayer began with words but dissolved into silent tears. Sometimes it was merely a one-word breath to heaven. Many times, I offered very simple prayers over my children, having no energy to pray at length or to describe what I was feeling: I just looked at my children and spoke their names back to the Father. Often I walked up to them while they were playing, touched their heads, and asked

God to bless their lives. I prayed constantly for Taylor's improvement and prayed the Lord would let his brothers turn out normal, perhaps even better because of their situation. I think back on those days and wonder if they had a clue why Mommy was touching their heads and whispering words under her breath.

Of course, I also always carried a prayer concern for my husband. *How will he bear this? How can he physically keep up?* I wondered. All I could do was ask God to bless him and strengthen him. He probably walked around wondering and praying the same things on my behalf.

God has taught me that he is faithful to answer all prayer over time. Some of those answers have taken years, but they did eventually come. Some answers are still in the making, but by faith I know they are coming. My husband has turned into a different man on many levels. Not a day goes by where I don't marvel at how God has moved in the lives of all my children. I am so proud of Taylor and his brothers, Terry and Tyler. The world might call us survivors, but God's Word calls us "overcomers" (1 John 5:4). We are overcoming daily by faith and now have something to offer the world—our profession of Christ and his faithfulness. I am reminded of a scripture passage from Psalm 66 that describes what God has done for my family through the heartache of autism.

> *For You, O God, have tested us;*
> *You have refined us as silver is refined.*
> *You brought us into the net;*
> *You laid affliction on our backs.*
> *You have caused men to ride over our heads;*
> *We went through fire and through water;*
> *But You brought us out to rich fulfillment.*
> *—Psalm 66:10–12*

Being the mother of a child with autism has also led me to a new level of growth, both emotionally and spiritually. I've learned to be humble, to seek God for everything, and to let go of what I cannot change. I've had to learn how to say no to requests that I clearly cannot do. (This I learned by trial and error, having gotten in over my head several times!) This was a hard process for me because I have various gifts and talents. I always thought a Christian woman should use her gifts and talents every time she is asked, but I found that time itself was no longer mine. Occasionally, people were puzzled when I had to back out of commitments or say no right at the outset. But I never meant to hurt anyone. The people asking me to serve had no clue what my life was really like, so it was up to me to decline. I suppose all women wish they could learn to say no sometimes, but I learned the hard way because my new lifestyle wouldn't permit me to overdo it. I could barely get my basic household chores done. Most of the time, I couldn't keep up and our house would be in shambles.

Autism taught me that there are many unexpected roles that we mothers might need to fill. I've joked that we are not special-needs mothers; we are professional jugglers in disguise. Most women say they are always changing hats and switching different roles during the day. The mother of a child with autism has a whole shelf of extra hats to put on. She must be wife, mother, therapist, researcher, and school advocate, as well as having to learn a great deal of medical lingo she didn't know existed. Many of my friends have remarked that I should have been a doctor, but I am no different than many other mothers of kids with autism. We have a lot of reading to do! Some mothers read magazines and cookbooks in their spare time, but mothers of children with autism read medical articles and lab reports till we're bleary-eyed. Sometimes we must turn off all thoughts of autism and focus on other people, ourselves, or other things. But our preoccupation with autism is quite possibly the hardest hat to take off.

If any of you lacks wisdom, let him ask of God,
who gives to all liberally and without reproach,
and it will be given to him.
—James 1:5

The mother of a child with autism becomes more sacrificial than she ever dreamed she could be. I realized early that the real me still existed but I had to give up parts of my life that I enjoyed. I've always been a highly creative person, doing all sorts of handicrafts at home. I had been a seamstress from my teens through my adult life up to that point. But after Taylor's diagnosis, I realized just how little extra time I had in my day. I had to give up those extras just to survive the roller coaster of daily life with autism. I put away the sewing machine, and I could rarely do crafts. However, God gave me a new gift and I began writing Christian poetry during the long hours of time alone with him when I could go nowhere else. Sometimes God inspired me with a theme or idea for a new poem during my wild, busy days; then I would awaken before my children and sit down to write the poem. I've shared this poetry to minister to other souls, and in turn God has been glorified through what I've learned in our suffering.

You might say my faith has been tested in regard to raising a child with a disability, but the challenges have also brought great blessings. I believe God used this disability to show me what only he could do, and many passages from his Word suddenly had new value to me. Bible passages that I barely noticed before now seemed like neon signs on the pages, meeting my deepest needs. Although I know the Bible was written for the entire world, at times a passage seemed to whisper, "This is for you, my child."

It's amazing how God can bless a mother with tender moments to end each long, difficult day. I treasured the moments after dark when Taylor would finally fall asleep. I felt he was somehow escaping autism while he slumbered. I wondered if he had pleasant dreams without the constraints of autism. For example, I wondered if he was able to talk in his dreams. I had my own dreams of his being able to talk, so I guessed he had them as well. Either way, I loved watching him lying there asleep. Many nights, I walked up to his little body, laying a hand on his back or shoulders and praying for God to touch him and heal his symptoms. Even now as he is older, I love the sight of him sleeping. *Sleep, dear Taylor, sleep.*

Children with autism can be very clumsy. Without their realizing it, they break a lot more things than normal kids do. I've endured the loss of many of my possessions over the years, becoming almost numb in the process. I experienced one of my greatest losses the day Taylor put my beautiful diamond wedding ring in the garbage disposal and turned it on. To this day I remember the awful clanking noise and the sight of my mangled ring. I thought I would suffocate when I saw it, realizing how costly it would be to fix. But in that heartsick moment, God reminded me that this world is not my home and that even heirlooms don't make it to the next one. His word was my only consolation that day. I was unable to make sense of it any other way.

> *For we brought nothing into this world,*
> *and it is certain we can carry nothing out.*
> *—1 Timothy 6:7*

Many people comment that they are encouraged by seeing that my personal faith in God is so strong. Rarely do they realize that God has used this journey to make it strong. Over the years, I have come to realize that true faith doesn't believe only when everything makes sense and flowers are blooming on the hillsides of normal life; faith must also believe during the days of senselessness. And believe me, nothing about autism makes much sense. There have been many exhausting days when I prayed for God's wisdom and endurance and for his touch on specific problems. During the early years, I frequently found myself praying for more faith, knowing deep down that faith was my most critical need.

Morning after morning, I rolled out of bed to face the same problems as the day before, but God never denied my request for increased faith. I always felt more confidence in God's help when I asked for it. Through faith, God revealed wisdom to me that I had never fully grasped before. When nothing in our lives was going well, I went to bed utterly exhausted but believing that God was still on the throne. Some nights when my head hit the pillow, I was so wiped out that I couldn't form any words to pray. In those moments, I simply looked up from my pillow and asked Jesus to pray over me. I know my Advocate did that as I drifted off into sleep.

"Peace I leave with you, My peace I give to you; not as the world gives do I give to you. Let not your heart be troubled, neither let it be afraid."
—*John 14:27*

Walking this unusual path has changed me spiritually for the better. For one thing, it has taught me to be less judgmental. I would have not thought myself judgmental before, but I must have been. Now, when another woman's child is throwing a tantrum for a candy bar in the grocery store, I do not stare or make remarks. For all I know, the child may have autism. The mother may be a struggling single parent, barely coping with her life. Because I have been that mother with a screaming kid myself, I know what it's like. I've come to look at all of life's heartaches with a new heart and am often able to see things others might miss. I've also come to look at other struggling souls who do not have Christ and ache for them, because their deepest need isn't to find a solution to their problems; it's the salvation of their souls. I have become doubly grateful that I have a King for my soul and a Shepherd to walk this difficult path alongside my family.

Autism has also taught me the power of forgiveness. Nobody likes to feel that others disapprove of their children, whether those children are normal or disabled. However, I have learned to forget the ugly remarks and stares we receive in public when Taylor does something unpredictable. Many children with autism have no physical marks or deformities that reveal they have a disability. Strangers look at a child who is acting out and then make a snap judgment about the child's parents, which is followed by cutting remarks or dirty looks. I have gently corrected a few people over the years when the situation merited it. But more often than not, I have accepted the remarks for what they are and forgiven the person, whether they spoke out of ignorance or judgmentalism. In the early years, when we ventured out in public with Taylor's erratic behavior, I didn't deal with people's remarks as well as I do now. I was a younger mother, so I took their comments personally as an attack on my parenting. But as I've grown into my role, I have learned that God will correct people over time, and he can do it in a way that is far more fitting than anything I could say. Autism's coverage by the news media in recent years has helped educate people on the disorder, and I've noticed a reduction in these kinds of incidents.

Autism has shown me that God can forgive me after I have messed up. I've seen his mercy thousands of times along this journey. When I think of autism and mercy, I am reminded of Sara. In the earliest years when I was so overwhelmed by Taylor's behaviors, a young girl by the name of Sara Lorenson showed up at my house. She knocked on the kitchen door and said she'd heard about Taylor and wanted to help me. I quickly told her she couldn't possibly handle him. I thanked her for her sweet offer as I sent her away. Several years later, I learned that Sara was studying to become a special-education teacher. Someone said I should call her to find out if she would be available to help with Taylor. I said to myself, *That's the girl I sent away!* But I called Sara and asked if she might do some respite care for us. She readily accepted and became a lifeline for us. I don't believe I would have survived some long summers without the breaks Sara gave me. I have to chuckle when I tell people that God gave Sara back to me after I goofed up and sent her away.

My friend Donna and I have both had people tell us that they could not do what we are doing. We know it's only because they haven't been presented with the same challenge we have; they really don't know what they could do. We believe that if God gave them a child with autism to raise, they would and could learn to do what we do. A tenacious love arrives the moment the diagnosis is made. We do what we must do. We get tired, overspent, and often teary-eyed. But we do it because our kids need us. There's an old saying most parents of children with disabilities hear: "God only gives special children to special parents." I dare to tweak that phrase a bit and say that God changes us into the parents we need to be to care for these kids. As the years rolled by, I knew God was changing me for the better.

To all the tired mothers of children with autism, I send a heartfelt blessing your way. God bless you all. I pray the love of Christ is your anchor and saving grace. Hang on, ladies. Help is coming your way.

Ministering to the Mother

Friendship

The mother of a child with autism desperately needs friendship. Her friends often disappear after the diagnosis simply because they didn't know how to redefine their relationship with her and can't cope with watching her family's pain. But I'm grateful to say I never had that problem.

The mother of a child with autism needs friendships to remain strong. She needs for her friends to realize that her life has changed dramatically. She may not be able to engage in the same girlfriend activities they used to enjoy together, and weekend trips to the mall may become a thing of the past, but she still needs their companionship.

Chances are that during the preschool years of a child with autism, the mother's friends will have to do more to maintain contact with her. If they used to meet every week at a bagel shop for their special time together, her friends may now need to come to her house and bring the bagels with them. They can offer to change things a bit in order for the mother not to feel guilty. Don't abandon your special times together; just remake them.

The mother's friends will learn that sometimes she needs to vent and unload all the stress she is carrying. She may talk in tears the entire time they are together. At other times, she may refrain from even speaking about the autism in order to take a mental break from it. Don't be afraid of her emotions. Women are expressive and we tend to talk when we are burdened. Getting those emotions out is like therapy for the mother, and I've done it numerous times with my friends. Most of them had no idea at the time how much they helped me just by listening. No lofty words of advice are needed, just a caring shoulder to lean on and two ears to listen.

Two are better than one,
Because they have a good reward for their labor.
For if they fall, one will lift up his companion.
But woe to him who is alone when he falls,
For he has no one to help him up.
—*Ecclesiastes 4:9–10*

Simple Acknowledgment of the Load She Bears

You can brighten the mother's day by the very simple act of sending her a card in the mail, acknowledging that you have noticed how much she does now and offering a few words of encouragement. I can't tell you how many times I convinced myself that people thought I was just like any other housewife and that they had no idea the strain I was under, and then a card would arrive, telling me that friends were praying for me because they knew that I was carrying a lot. Sometimes, the simplest words encouraged me the most.

Honor her on Mother's Day. We may be in the habit of honoring our own mothers on Mother's Day, but it is a perfect opportunity to find a special card to honor the mother of a child with autism. When you sign it, mention your awareness of her extraordinary role in raising a child with autism. If her child is very young or nonverbal, this gesture is even more appropriate.

Respite from the Physical Stress

The mother of a child with autism needs a break more often than she gets. I've never spoken to any mother of a child with autism who doesn't express total exhaustion. Many of them have at least one person trained to watch their children, but most do not have as much help as they need. This is where you or your church could become involved.

Watching a child with autism is different from caring for other children, but it's not impossible. It does require more forethought. For example, it requires getting to know the child *before* the need arises. In an emergency, it is not wise for the parents of a child with autism to call someone who has never sat with the child and ask them to come over. The sitter needs to make several visits to the home to see how the child performs and moves around in his or her own environment. Just come over for casual visits over coffee or tea, watching carefully all the while what goes on in the home. This is as much for the child as it is for you, because the autistic child needs to be comfortable with you as well. Pay close attention to the child's habits and how the mother handles them. Ask any questions that come to mind as you make your visits.

Most children with autism have favorite TV shows, which you need to know. Never argue with a child with autism when it's time for the daily ritual of his or her favorite TV program! Favorite foods and preparation methods are important to know as well. Children with autism are usually rigid with their schedules. They find change downright painful and difficult to handle. However, most mothers of children with autism will prepare well-written instructions for any caregiver who watches their children.

My recommendation is that you test the waters by watching the child for thirty minutes the first time, with the mother staying close by, within reach of her cell phone. If that goes well, increase the time span a little on your second assignment as you are comfortable. Eventually, the mother can be gone for a few hours and you will get the blessing of providing her with a well-deserved break.

More than one person in your congregation should become involved in respite care (baby-sitting) for the child. There are men in every congregation who are good with children, and this would be a great time to enlist them in helping out. Children with autism often respond well to men. Husband-wife teams make great sitters too. Even teenagers can help, coming in pairs and watching the child together after they have been well trained. Another idea is to spread the word to the closest colleges. Many colleges have students majoring in special education who would love the opportunity to get to know a child with autism before they enter that field.

I consider respite care one of the most important things that can be done to benefit the mother of a child with autism. So many things hinge on the availability of capable sitters. This is also your opportunity to get to know her child better. Just by seeing how physically demanding her job is, you will become better able to minister to her in other ways. It will also give you a deeper understanding of how you can pray for the entire family.

It's one thing to hear a prayer request spoken about a family dealing with autism; it's quite another to step into the home and see exactly what autism is like behind closed doors.

Warm Food to Comfort Body and Soul
Never underestimate the value of a hot meal. If this is the only thing you can do for a family dealing with autism, you will still be helping a great deal. Home-cooked food has a healing quality. I could have written a cookbook from all the wonderful meals brought to our house! More often than not, the stressed-out mother cannot cook as she would like. Days roll by as the mother deals with her child's autism and the many appointments; supper preparation gets pushed aside and forgotten. She may go for days on instant or quick foods just to get by.

Tips for the Gift of Meals
- Make a double recipe the next time you prepare your favorite casserole. Call the mother of a child with autism and tell her she can bake it or put it in her freezer for a day when she is too busy to cook. She will love just knowing that it's there for back-up.

- If possible, create a meal with recyclable containers or throwaway dishes, to lessen the duty of returning dishes.

- Enlist the retired generation of your church for the ministry of meal preparation. Many of them feel physically unable to perform respite care for the child, but they would jump at the chance to prepare a home-cooked meal.

- Bless the autistic child's family with gift cards to their favorite restaurant or pizza place. Many of these families must forego eating out but would treasure the gift of take-out food.

- Create a package gift in which one couple from your church buys the parents' supper and another provides (or pays for) respite care for the evening so that the parents can go out by themselves.

Relieving Stress in the Mother's Week
While this tip may seem like a no-brainer, it is worthy of thought: Ask the mother if there is a situation during the week that causes her a great deal

of stress. Is there an afternoon when her other children must be taken to music or sports practice? Perhaps the loading and unloading of her child with autism to attend to that one duty is extremely stressful. Your assistance in a situation like that could greatly help, reducing the mother's stress level.

This is another ministry that retired couples or people with grown children would love to help with. People often don't know what to do, but they would relish the idea of doing something simple every week to assist the family.

Moving the Mountain of the Mundane

To say that housework falls behind due to autism is an understatement! I recall being exhausted by the end of the afternoon. And then after supper, it was time to chase Taylor all over again. The supper dishes often sat on the counter all night, greeting me at sunrise, waiting for the next snatch of time that came up.

Several precious souls came to clean my house and help me get caught up. My mother came on a regular basis in the early years of Taylor's autism, staying the entire day doing the grubbiest jobs in the house. (I think the Lord probably has a special crown in heaven for her. Maybe it's called the housecleaning crown. We will find out when God hands out the crowns!)

It may not be possible for you to devote several hours to housecleaning, but if God calls you to do it, you will know. This may be something you could offer to do sporadically when you have time off—or something you do on a regular basis as your offering to the family.

Other Housecleaning Ideas

- Ask the mother of a child with autism what day she likes to catch up with her housecleaning and then come help tend her children while she works. This will maximize the work she gets done on her cleaning day.

- Do you have a gift with organizing? Call the mother and offer to clean and organize an area of her home that is bothering her the most. It could be a walk-in closet, her kitchen cabinets, or some other area. Go in and work on it while she's there so she can tell you what needs kept or gotten rid of.

- Do you happen to know some of her other friends? A group of women could pool their energy and come to her house on the same day for a housecleaning party. Multiple people would maximize the work accomplished. In addition to the relief of seeing her housework caught up, she would be thrilled by the company of her friends.

- Are you cleaning your own house and preparing to take a load of things to charity? Call the mother of a child with autism and ask if she has unwanted items she would like picked up as well. You'd be surprised how many times she cannot do little tasks like this, due to caring for her child's basic needs. This has been done for me, and it helps so much to free up space.

Restoring Some of Her Former Life

It's no secret that mothers of children with autism give up a great deal to be the mothers they need to be. Most will not speak of their losses because it hurts too much. The gifts, talents, and experiences they enjoyed before autism are now gone because their lives have been turned upside-down to focus on a little child in pain.

Perhaps you could restore some of a mother's former life by reestablishing one thing she misses the most. You cannot restore everything, of course, but one thing could bless her and create a day of the week she looks forward to with anticipation. Many times a mother who has trained respite providers will not think to use them so she can do something for herself. Did she love aerobics class or singing in the local choir? Is she a budding artist who would like to go back to art class? This is the perfect opportunity to see if you or someone else could fill in for her so she could do something for herself each week. She will come back home grateful, refreshed, and feeling like she is still a person with her own interests and desires.

Pampering Does a Body Good

Does she need some pampering? If she hasn't had time or money to do her nails in a long while, bring a friend to watch the children while you do her nails. If someone in your church is a hairstylist, offer to provide a haircut or other service to refresh the mother.

Gift certificates for a professional massage would be wonderful. The mother's shoulders often seem to carry the weight of the world, and her muscles have a way of fighting back when they do too much.

Think Outside the Box

Because everyone is unique, we all have special gifts and talents to offer. Are you good at something creative? Perhaps you are talented at scrapbooking or home decorating. Most mothers of children with autism run behind on things such as scrapbooking for their kids, just because they have no spare time. Offer to pick up her family photos and create scrapbook pages for her. The mother could pay you for the materials, but your labor could be a gift of love she would treasure.

Home decorating is something women generally love. We enjoy seeing new pictures on the wall or furniture placed in new and creative ways. If you have a knack for this kind of thing, let the mother know you are available and would love to help. It could be as simple as helping to arrange a grouping of new photos of her kids or rearrange her furniture after spring cleaning. Whatever your special gifts are, use them for service.

Seasonal Help for the Mother

Any task like window washing or planting flowers could be a welcome gift of service for the mother of a child with autism. Ask her what she loves to do for the holidays but can't seem to get to. Gift wrapping at Christmas is a great thing to offer, especially if the mother has other children and lots of things to wrap. (Some of these tasks can be assigned to your church youth group as a means of teaching them how to serve.)

Do you love to bake? Contact the mother before the Christmas season and let her know you can help her with baking if need be. Frequently, the mother of a child with autism needs help with the simple things, like making cupcakes for their children's school parties. What seems impossible for her might be right up your alley.

Helping Her with the Impossible

Perhaps after you've gotten to know the family of a child with autism and learned of their biggest battles, God will lay something unusual on your heart. It may be something I've not mentioned here. Keep your heart open to whatever the Lord might lead you to do.

When I think of the impossible, I remember Donetta Murray, Taylor's aide from public school. Donetta became very concerned that Taylor was not potty trained. The fact that my attempts at potty training efforts had been fruitless made me want to give up in exhaustion; I lost heart. Donetta made it her mission and didn't give up until we saw progress. She sat for hours on the bathroom floor with little treats to reward Taylor for his efforts. Her determination created a victory that made me feel like there was hope after all. Taylor was potty trained by the first grade, and I often wonder whether it would have happened had Donetta not responded in the way she did.

When you come into the home of friends dealing with autism, be open to the unusual. You may end up being a conduit of blessing that they will remember for years to come.

Now may our God and Father Himself, and our Lord Jesus Christ, direct our way to you. And may the Lord make you increase and abound in love to one another and to all, just as we do to you, so that He may establish your hearts blameless in holiness before our God and Father at the coming of our Lord Jesus Christ with all His saints.
—1 Thessalonians 3:11–13

CHAPTER 3

From the Father's Side of the Table

Being a woman limits me somewhat in this chapter. While it is not hard to describe what autism does to a mother, both emotionally and physically, it is a bit harder for me to describe it from a man's point of view. But I can tell you what I've seen in the life of my husband.

It was only weeks after Taylor's diagnosis that I discovered my husband Bret on the bed looking at Taylor with teary eyes. He said, "I keep asking myself, *Why him? Why him?*" I don't recall my answer, but I remember the question as if it was yesterday. It held all the emotion of a father who was hanging on for dear life and asking questions that had no real answers this side of eternity.

Bret later shared with me that he retreated into denial for a while after our son's diagnosis because it seemed more comfortable to do so. He was quiet and almost detached from the busyness that was going on, but I was perhaps so busy myself that I didn't see it as denial. While I dug into research and a brand-new style of mothering, my husband was secretly hoping it would all go away. After he accepted the reality of Taylor's disorder, he believed there had to be some sort of medical treatment to create an instant fix. It was as if Bret was letting God know he would believe the autism was real if there was a patch to repair the hole that was widening in our lives.

When a man discovers his child has autism, he feels devastated. He questions himself in the same ways the mother does, but he internalizes things much more. He almost has to do that, simply to survive and keep going. Most mothers become the caregivers while the fathers try to keep the family afloat financially. The father has to go to work and try to keep his thoughts focused enough to do his job, all the while secretly wondering what's going on at his house. *Is this a bad day? How is it going back at home? Is she going to be able to handle all she's doing? Where will we be ten years from now?* All these are thoughts the man has during his day. It's not an easy task to balance it all in his mind, so men often find themselves hurting in ways they can't express.

My husband carried a private grief for years over the what-ifs and what-if-nots of our son's autism. The hardest part was sorting out what to do with the grief and how to even put it into words. Grief is an emotion that we can experience for reasons other than death. Any major loss can result in grief. Fathers of children with autism have to grieve the loss of what they felt would be a normal future for their child. Because autism is four times more likely in boys, the majority of children with autism are male. There's not a man alive who doesn't dream of his little boy doing "man things." He hopes to have a companion at ballgames, a young competitor in sports, or just another male friend to take a walk with. If the child is a girl, he is saddened by the loss of her possibilities; in all likelihood, she will not get married and have children. All daddies dream of walking their daughters down the aisle on their wedding day. But autism changes all that and leaves a father searching his heart for the right way to digest the pain and grieve the losses. He has no clue how much of the autism can be overcome and how much will truly be a lifelong loss. It's difficult to grieve something whose outcome you can't quite foresee, and men often have trouble expressing their pain anyway. But the grief resulting from the autism is there, no matter what. My husband says, "I assumed when Taylor was born that I would involve him in sports with his big brother Tyler. It didn't take long to realize that I would not be coaching any ball teams for Taylor."

As the years progressed, Bret realized the gravity of our son's disability. He pondered the scheme of life and quietly asked God, "Why did this happen to my family?" In the previous chapter, I shared how I had walked through a season of false guilt regarding our son's diagnosis because I had not taken prenatal vitamins before his birth. Bret did the same thing, but in a different way. He secretly questioned his personal faith. He wondered if some sin in his past was to blame for our son's diagnosis. Later on, God broke through and gave my husband the heart-rescue he needed. Bret shares this comment: "The bottom line is that God does allow bad things to happen to good people. We have to rely on that faith in God that He will be there for us when we need that strength. He is sovereign and in control and will bring us through everything."

I would have lost heart, unless I had believed
That I would see the goodness of the LORD
In the land of the living.
—Psalm 27:13

Now men like to play the role of problem solvers in most families. It's just part of their nature. But men who expect to analyze and fix every problem that comes along will likely struggle with the issue of autism. Most men have never seen autism up close and personal before. They can't create an instant game plan to win this conflict, and they may not know exactly what to do, at least at the onset. The sense of helplessness may lead a father into a season of depression. Each father is different in how he digests the autism diagnosis in his family. Although there are many different ways to deal with the diagnosis, some are emotionally far healthier for the father. My husband shares that if he thought about Taylor's autism for too long, then panic and fear set in. He had to take his mind elsewhere in order to cope. I often felt that Bret was not listening to me and what I had to share about Taylor's problems; this was the reason why. I was in command mode while he was trying to escape the feelings of helplessness that haunted his thoughts. I was proactive while he was reactive, having nowhere to hide.

In addition to the emotional strain a father normally experiences with a disabled child, autism renders many mothers unable to work outside the home. I've met women with full-time professional careers who had to quit their jobs in order to take on the full-time job of caring for a child with autism. Sometimes, mothers are able to remake their careers into part-time assignments, tailoring their time around the needs of the child. But the role of caregiver is usually so time-consuming and exhaustive that it eliminates that possibility. My husband Bret remarked numerous times that, even though we really could have used the money, he knew I couldn't hold down a job on top of what I was already doing. There are doctor's appointments, updates to write, daily supplements to administer and keep on hand, along with special school meetings to attend. And all of this is on top of basic housekeeping. Someone has to be in charge of the care of the child with autism, and someone must be physically at home with the child. At our house the problem was compounded by Taylor's addiction to me. I call it an addiction because it wouldn't do it justice to call our relationship an "attachment." He simply had to have me near him at all times. Taylor would throw lengthy tantrums when I was absent, leaving Bret baffled at how to give me a break so that I could get away for a while. And if I wasn't home when Taylor got off the bus, nobody wanted to be the one standing at the end of our driveway to meet him. This addiction can still flare up when Taylor spends too much time at home with me. This problem, combined with the fact that few people could handle Taylor, essentially eliminated the possibility of my working outside the home.

None of these limitations on employment can be helped. They are part of the package of autism, leaving many households that formerly had two incomes with less money for living expenses. As a result of the financial distress, some husbands take on extra duties to earn money to keep bills paid. My husband was one of them. My husband Bret has officiated sports for years. Many people believe he does it because he loves sports, and that was the case when he first began, but now he continues to officiate because we need the money. His body has become tired of it, but the checkbook says he can't quit. That black-and-white striped shirt sometimes means the difference between having enough to pay the bills or running out of groceries. He comes home totally exhausted after ball games, but the extra money in his pocket makes him feel better about our finances. There was a year where I begged Bret to stop officiating games because I was so overwhelmed at home. But we realized how badly we needed that bit of extra money, so he returned to his referee jobs the next year.

The extra expenses connected to autism will weigh on the father who feels he must be the family's breadwinner. If he isn't struggling to learn what autism is, he is struggling to learn how to pay for it. Medical bills loom over his head like a cloud that won't go away. Not only does he have a wife who can't hold an outside job, but now he has a child with unreal medical expenses. Children with autism undergo medical tests that are often quite expensive. While some families use insurance or medical aid programs to pay those bills, other families do not qualify for such aid. Some states have programs or grants that help pay for these services, but they are often limited; many states have waiting lists that are years long due to the increasing prevalence of autism. In addition, many families, like ours, choose to use natural treatments for autism. These are rarely covered by any insurance, although they are very costly. So the father of a child with autism is torn between the need to pay increasing bills and the need to stay at home to relieve the exhausted mother.

My husband says that learning to deal with the financial unpredictability of autism has been one of the largest personal hurdles he has overcome. Bret is a banker, and over the years he has seen a variety of instances where failure to manage money caused families to break and sometimes fail. That set the tone for a vow he made within himself. He always said that when he had a wife and kids and dealt with his own family finances, all his financial "ducks" would be in a row. He vowed he would not repeat mistakes he had seen in others. He had no idea what autism would do to that vow, and he humbly had to admit that he was in uncharted territory.

My husband and I have differing opinions on finances, and it has come out in occasional disagreements. He had a habit of stewing and fretting over the bills, while I kept reassuring him that God would provide. It was very hard for him to apply his faith to our family finances, the one area that he always said he would keep under control. Even so, as strained as our family has been over the years, God always came through before the worst happened. My husband now says, "It is comforting to know God as the Great Provider." God always did as he said he would do.

Give us this day our daily bread.
—Matthew 6:11

My husband and I both know there are times when the other one needs some space. For example, I know to stay away when he's trying to pay bills. When I see him with a stack of papers and running his fingers through his hair while writing checks, that's my cue to reduce stress in the room. Often, I will literally take charge and attend to everything our sons need during that time in order to eliminate any noise or disruptions. We have an unspoken understanding in our marriage: I work on all the details directly connected to Taylor's autism while Bret finds ways to pay for all of it. We've divided the duties the only way we know how. Although I've joked over the years that he could never do my job, I know beyond all doubt that I'd never want his, either. People have frequently asked my husband how he continues doing what he does, because they see the sacrifice and physical strain. There are no easy ways for fathers to do all they must do, but pure love for their child keeps them going. They might not understand all the whys of their lives or the autism, but they completely understand the love they hold in their hearts for their children. Love drives them to do what they do in the midst of the unknown.

> *As a father pities his children,*
> *So the* LORD *pities those who fear Him.*
> —*Psalm 103:13*

My husband and I also found that God has a way of having us help each other. I might have a weakness in an area of parenting where Bret has a great strength. Sometimes this means I need to become strong in that area; but at other times, we just accept that God made us uniquely different in ways that work to our mutual benefit. I've always tumbled into bed hours before my husband. I am definitely a morning person, while Bret is a night person. As I pray in the mornings, I have often wondered how many concerns Bret lays before God in those hours alone when he is awake while the rest of the family sleeps. We used to think we were a mismatch because our body clocks were opposite. But Bret and I came to realize that if we hadn't been on different sleep cycles, we could not have taken shifts during the all-night spells when Taylor didn't sleep at all. God always knows what He is doing, even as He creates our internal body rhythms.

> *My eyes are awake through the night watches,*
> *That I may meditate on Your word.*
> *Hear my voice according to Your lovingkindness;*
> *O* LORD, *revive me according to Your justice.*
> —*Psalm 119:148–49*

Sometimes fathers of children with autism are a bit intimidated to realize all that their wives have come to understand about autism but which they have yet to learn. Most mothers of children with autism have an unusual intuition. I've seen it in nearly every case of autism I've observed personally. Granted, God places intuition in all mothers, but I believe it is heightened when a child has autism. Fathers often have to learn intuitive insights from their wives as they go along. Until then, they may not know exactly what to do when they are alone with the child.

One time Taylor was going berserk over something in the living room while I was in the kitchen cooking supper with my back turned. Bret asked what in the world could be wrong with him. I told him that the knob had probably fallen off the TV and that he should look for it on the floor behind the television set. Later, after the situation had been resolved, Bret asked how I knew what had upset Taylor without even being in the room. I told him it was the sound of Taylor's cry; that was how he cried when the TV knob fell off. Bret raised his eyebrows and seemed genuinely baffled. He may have wondered how he could ever learn the sound of a cry and know its root cause. But he has come to know plenty over the years, as we've gone to the school of autism together. We have learned the same lessons differently, but we have had the same Teacher.

> *Have you not known?*
> *Have you not heard?*
> *The everlasting God, the* LORD,
> *The Creator of the ends of the earth,*
> *Neither faints nor is weary.*
> *His understanding is unsearchable.*
> *He gives power to the weak,*
> *And to those who have no might He increases strength.*
> *Even the youths shall faint and be weary,*
> *And the young men shall utterly fall,*
> *But those who wait on the* LORD
> *Shall renew their strength;*
> *They shall mount up with wings like eagles,*
> *They shall run and not be weary,*
> *They shall walk and not faint.*
> —Isaiah 40:28–31

The caregiver spotlight usually falls on the mother, simply because outsiders see the mother so often with the child with autism. This is why I've been praised considerably over the years for all I do with my son. But I honestly don't think people have seen the strain and sacrifice my husband has borne. He has done a fantastic job. Coping with our son's disorder has polished my husband's personality, and I've noticed that other fathers of children with autism have similar qualities. My husband is much more tender and less rough around the edges. Perhaps autism has softened him until all the macho stuff has been worn off. Bret laughs and says, "I don't think I have any pride left at all." Autism has taught him humility as we've had to seek God in desperation over so many issues, but also as we have gotten to see God's glory in his provisions along the way. I would say that Bret's personality, which was already good, has become great in the years of dealing with autism. My husband's expressive side has been heightened by being Taylor's dad. He is not afraid to kiss Taylor in public, and he seems more expressive of his other feelings than he used to be. From where I sit, my husband seems more balanced and more focused on what is really important in life.

The righteous man walks in his integrity;
His children are blessed after him.
—*Proverbs 20:7*

The same pride and love he holds for our other children, Bret holds for Taylor as well. The others might be praised for sports accomplishments or college awards, while Taylor is praised for learning to wait at a restaurant for his food. Bret is genuinely proud of all three of our sons. Fathers of children with autism can be torn just like the mother is in regard to spending time equally with the children of the household. Any siblings in the household will have competing desires and needs, which is more difficult to manage when one of them is a child with autism who needs extra attention every day of the week. Bret learned over time to balance his special-needs fathering with the fathering of our other sons. Spending quality time with our other sons was one of the more difficult lessons Bret had to master. Sometimes mothers and fathers take turns giving the other children individual attention, and this is what we had to do. Bret might take our son Tyler to sports events by himself, while he tags me to take Tyler for shopping days alone. I don't like missing the games at all, but I treasure the time we spend shopping, so it works for us. We take what we can get and try to enjoy the part that is ours. Other parents may say this is not normal, but it's the only life we've known for years.

One day Bret shared how drastically his life had changed in a few short years after marrying me: "I was thirty-three years old when I got married and immediately became a stepfather to my son Terry. To our surprise, Tyler was born nine months after the wedding, and Taylor's birth followed fifteen months after Tyler's. In the space of twenty-four months, I became a husband, stepfather, father, and then a special-needs father. It is probably good that I didn't get married until my thirties. I probably couldn't have handled the changes that happened so quickly if I had still been in my twenties."

Autism can add considerable stress to a marriage. The marital relationship might be on the back burner for some very good reasons. Although the woman is doing what she's supposed to do by caring for their child with autism, that intensive care-giving role will cut into marital time and attention. It really can't be helped, but it adds an element of stress to a marriage that must be recognized. The husband married a woman he loves, but she becomes a tired and overspent woman in the wake of the responsibilities of autism. For many years, I fell asleep on the couch before the sun went down in the evening. When I sat down, I quickly slumped over into a ball and dozed off. I didn't even have enough energy to ask how Bret's day had been. I was just grateful he was home and that another set of hands was in the house to help. My husband never complained, but I know he felt a sense of loneliness at times.

Because of Taylor's autism, my husband and I rarely have private time together. We've never been on a weekend trip alone since Taylor was born, and we consider our anniversary night out at a restaurant to be a big deal. Despite all that, our marriage has stood the test of time. We've discovered that special trips do not strengthen a marriage; only God does that. At times, we ache for what other married couples have, but we always realize that some aspects of our situation cannot be changed, so we go on. We'd rather have Taylor than a normal marriage, and we know that God has placed him into our marriage for a reason. There is a gentle peace in bowing to God's plans, even when they make no sense to the mortal mind.

The trials and heartaches of autism can strengthen the spiritual heart of a man. I've watched my husband's personal relationship with Christ continue to grow, despite the adversities of autism. He openly professes God's faithfulness and believes in God's promises for our family much more than he used to. Sure, there have been times when he has become low emotionally from the stress, but in the end, he has become stronger spiritually than before. Some people talk a lot about their faith, while others simply live it, placing one foot in front of the other. My husband lives his faith. At times we've felt our marriage was being tested, but we know we have been refined for eternal purposes. Often, we had to trust God to guide us through an ordeal we were facing.

> *Behold, I have refined you, but not as silver;*
> *I have tested you in the furnace of affliction.*
> *For My own sake, for My own sake, I will do it;*
> *For how should My name be profaned?*
> *And I will not give My glory to another.*
> —Isaiah 48:10–11

Men who have children with autism must juggle their schedules, just as their wives do. They too can fall behind on their chores around the house. Children with autism must always be monitored and supervised, even while they are in the house. They literally have to be watched at all times. Most children gradually mature and can be left in the house alone while a parent is working outside. Not so with a child who has autism. Often, the child's mother waits until the father comes home each day so she can do things she needs to do, such as run to the store, get a haircut, or cook supper. The child with autism is basically handed over in shifts. My husband can't mow the lawn and leave our son in the house if I am not there. Sometimes Bret flies in the door after work, ready to do yard work, when I remind him of an appointment I had. That means he isn't going to get his chores done after all. It's really a balancing act every day of the week.

While my husband privately wrestled with God at the onset of our journey with autism, he came to see that his faith in God was more than enough to get him through as a man and a father. For many years, I told Bret that God had a plan for our lives that included Taylor's autism. In the earliest years, Bret had a difficult time believing that autism could be part of a divine plan, but God brought him full circle to the day when he offered me this quote: "Even though autism in the family creates many problems; physically, emotionally, and spiritually, I feel I am a better person for having lived through all the trials and tribulations. I feel blessed to be the father of an autistic son, Taylor, whom I love very much and consider just as precious as any normal child."

Honestly, the fathers of children with autism deserve medals for their roles as fathers, just as much as the mothers do for their mothering. They might well be the unsung heroes of autism. God bless Bret and all the tired daddies of children with autism.

Ministering to the Father

Friendship and Brotherhood

Fathers of children with autism need friendships in much the same way women do. While women are used to pouring out their hearts to their confidantes, men often are not. The father needs friends who will check on his emotional condition from week to week. The father may not be able to talk very much about what's on his heart and will only answer in short responses, but a wise friend will realize that even these short responses may lead to the day when the father will reach out to him and pour out everything he has bottled up. So, a constant friendship will bless the father.

Men are sometimes overly worried that they don't have good advice to give each other for their problems. Sage advice for parenting a child with autism cannot be pulled out of a hat, so don't worry about that. If you have a friend who's the father of a child with autism, don't avoid him for these reasons. This is the time to remain close and be the friend who gets him through the tough times.

Phone him during those stretches of time when you can't see him in person. Just knowing his friends are a phone call away will give him comfort. Sometimes, phone calls aren't possible and e-mail can be used. I would refrain from using e-mail for all your contacts, but at times it can be used to check on the father if he is at work all day. In addition, some men find that writing about their feelings is easier than speaking about them. In this way, e-mail could be beneficial.

A man who has friends must himself be friendly,
But there is a friend who sticks closer than a brother.
—Proverbs 18:24

A Weekend Outing to Refresh His Spirit

If possible and with his wife's assistance, plan a men's outing with your friend for a Saturday. Perhaps you might invite another friend or two whom the father hasn't seen for a while, which will make the outing more meaningful. If his wife knows what you are planning to do, she may be able to line up extra help for herself to get through the weekend. She will be touched that you are reaching out to her husband. He needs time away from the stress as much as she does; he needs a break now and then.

Be kindly affectionate to one another with brotherly love, in honor giving preference to one another; not lagging in diligence, fervent in spirit, serving the Lord; rejoicing in hope, patient in tribulation, continuing steadfastly in prayer; distributing to the needs of the saints, given to hospitality.
—Romans 12:10–13

Men Need Prayer Support

Men need men who will pray over them. We've gotten away from praying over each other in the body of Christ. We offer to post names on prayer lists or say that we will keep each other in prayer. But it's amazingly healing to actually hear someone praying over you, to hear the words being offered up to the Lord on your behalf. The father of a child with autism needs to realize that he need not rely on his strength alone; his strength will come from the power of God. Those audible prayers can fuel a father for days afterward. He may shed a few tears in the moment, but they will be good for him. My husband has had a few men pray over him, and he's remarked how much it meant to him. I could see a visible difference in his demeanor after they prayed with him.

The Father May Need Physical Help with the Chores

As mentioned earlier, the father of a child with autism often falls behind on his household duties. You or the men of your church might be able to step in and help. Approach him several weeks ahead of time and offer to come on a Saturday to help him catch up. This way, he can think of what needs to be done the most and be ready. You may want to focus on the fellowship aspect of your visit, letting the father know you want to be with him and help him at the same time. This is especially important until he gets used to the idea of accepting help. Later, he will more readily gain the blessing of male bonding and having his work caught up periodically. Your congregation will be blessed to know you were able to do something to assist him.

Seasonal Work Always Comes Due

Seasonal work often lags behind in households dealing with autism. Youth groups could find this a valuable ministry to the family. Teens could spend an afternoon raking leaves or helping clean out a garage for the father. The siblings in the family would also see young people serving and would learn a spiritual lesson from it.

The father may need help with the monumental task of completing his taxes each year. Do you have someone in your congregation who is good at accounting? This could be an act of service he or she could perform for the family. Any seasonal help of this kind could help to relieve stress for the father.

The Large and Daunting Task of Painting

I can safely say that painting the walls is impossible at our house. If you think painting at your house is a job, imagine painting a room with a child with autism teetering near the ladder and eyeballing the paint. Does the family lament how much they need to have their house painted? Families of children with autism stay home more than others and see those scuffed walls constantly. This could be another area of ministry. There are probably people in your church who are handy at painting. Ask around to discover who they are. Several people could accomplish in a weekend what the family of a child with autism could never get done.

My sister and her husband did this for my family one summer. It was so refreshing to see newly painted walls after they had been scuffed up for so long. It was like getting a new house and a fresh start. My husband and I will never forget their labor of love. Any large task like painting, carpet cleaning, or basement cleaning could be an area of ministry to the father. Keep your eyes open for ways you can help him.

Restoring Some of His Former Life

Just as the mother of a child with autism gives up a great deal of her life, so does the father. Find out what he misses the most. Perhaps restoring some aspect of his former life will lift his spirits and make him feel like he is still the man he used to be.

Did he used to coach Little League and have to give it up? Perhaps by assisting the mother each week at the ballpark, you could enable him to return to coaching. Did he go to the gym a few times a week? Fathers of children with autism start skipping their own activities to stay at home and assist the mother. Perhaps you could come to the home and help the mother on evenings he goes to the gym. He may have neglected himself simply because finances are so tight. If so, you or a group of people could provide a gift card for his favorite activity. Take time to listen to his heart. Sooner or later, you will discover something you can do to help him recover a part of himself.

Therefore if there is any consolation in Christ, if any comfort of love, if any fellowship of the Spirit, if any affection and mercy, fulfill my joy by being like-minded, having the same love, being of one accord, of one mind. Let nothing be done through selfish ambition or conceit, but in lowliness of mind let each esteem others better than himself. Let each of you look out not only for his own interests, but also for the interests of others.
—*Philippians 2:1–4*

CHAPTER 4
The Siblings' Point of View

O ne day, a Judevine[1] technician named Ruth Wood was at my kitchen table working with Taylor. As she worked, we also discussed the ways in which autism affects a family. Ruth informed me in a very sweet but convincing way that my other children would be impacted greatly in the years to come because of Taylor's autism. At the time Taylor was about four, Tyler was five, and our oldest son, Terry, was fourteen. The expression on her face caught me off guard and caused me to think for a long time about her remark. It didn't take long to realize that she was absolutely right. Our other children have been affected in every way imaginable due to their brother's autism.

My husband and I have often reflected on the upside-down nature of our household. We both had very normal childhoods, but our kids have grown up with no clue about what normal is really like. Tyler is only fifteen months older than Taylor, so he has always known a family with an autistic sibling. At times I wonder if his future wife will have to educate him about what normal family life is like. I hope that he can find it in his heart to let her teach him, and I hope she is patient with him. She has no idea that I am praying for her already, and I don't even know who she is. We will know her when we see her, for she will likely be the most patient young woman on earth.

---

1. Judevine Center for Autism is dedicated to helping young people with autism enter the mainstream of community life. Judevine has several offices in Missouri.

Terry was ten years old when Taylor was born, and that ten-year difference sometimes helped him cope with the autism a little better than Tyler
does. When Taylor's autism was beginning to take an emotional toll on
the family, Terry was old enough to drive, so he could leave the house to
escape the devastation. He always had to come back home, though, and
he returned to a frazzled mother, a worn-out dad, and a little brother who
screamed at the slightest thing that went wrong. We realized along the line
that Terry needed privacy and a break from the strain, so we built him a
new bedroom in the basement of our house, and he spent many long hours
in there. I often wanted to hide in his room with him and talk about life, but
my duties with Taylor kept me from it. My visits to Terry's room in those
teenage years were few and far between. Also due to the age difference,
Terry had a more developed mind and could think of the future in ways
that his younger brother Tyler probably didn't. Terry probably had some
pretty serious concerns that he kept to himself. I think he worried for both
his mom and stepfather, wondering how much we could take of the bizarre
situation that unfolded a little more with each passing year.

Although Terry's losses might have been mitigated by his maturity,
there is no doubt that he suffered as well. He began realizing early in the
throes of Taylor's autism that he couldn't have his mother's attention as
much as before. I tried hard to make up the differences when I could, but
there was a shortage of attention that I just couldn't help. As a mother, I
felt another kind of pain when Terry was in his college years. I've always
been the homemaker type who bakes cookies and attends school parties.
But when Terry was in college, I was so tied to Taylor's needs that I couldn't
drive to his campus and visit him. I wanted so badly just to make a batch of
cookies and surprise him with a visit, but I couldn't get there and back by
the end of Taylor's school day. I saw Terry's college only two times while
he was enrolled there—the day I took him as a prospective student to tour
the college and the day he graduated. Visiting Terry with his classmates
was a secret longing of my heart, and I shed quiet tears when I thought
about it. I missed him so badly during that time. Somehow I knew Terry
wanted those visits too. A look in his eyes signaled the pain he was carrying. Yet, by God's grace, we both got through those years. Terry has never
discussed the emotional losses that autism brought to him, but I know
those losses exist.

Terry is now a married man, wedded in 2006 to a lovely young lady named Stephanie Moss. Stephanie is a quiet little soul who must be surprised at all the racket in our house. She seems to take it all in stride, though. My heart smiles at the very sight of her walking in my door. She's part of my answered prayers for Terry during all those years, that God would reward his life with happiness and normalcy. *Thank you God, for Stephanie.*

Terry and Tyler had to learn that our family life was altered in ways that other families might never encounter. If one of our children needed to purchase supplies for a class project, we had to find somewhere to leave Taylor or we had to wait until his father got home to watch him. We rarely ever took Taylor on a trip to a store where we needed to find things and ponder buying decisions. Taylor was far too unpredictable for that. Either his patience would wear out too soon or his obsessions would dictate the aisles where we could look. We have jokingly said that every errand for our family requires an act of Congress. While that seems like an exaggeration, compared to normal families, it wasn't an exaggeration at all. For all that we've been through, we believe our kids have turned out pretty well.

And we know that all things work together for good to those who love God, to those who are the called according to His purpose.
—Romans 8:28

Children with autistic siblings learn there are situations where they simply can't have both parents at the same time. One parent is with them and the other is caring for their autistic sibling. At times, we had to make choices that were just not fair. I recall the summer our son Tyler wanted my husband to be his baseball coach. I reminded him that when his daddy had done that a few summers before, I was unable to attend many of the ballgames because I had to chase his brother all over the ballpark by myself. I gently tried to convince Tyler that it would be better if someone else coached his team so that both parents could attend more of his games. Tyler persisted until one day he said, "Mom, it's not that I don't want you at my ballgames; it's just that I love having dad as my coach." Suddenly, I realized the decision he faced. One look into that precious face and I knew I had to yield. He was just being a normal boy who wanted his own dad to coach his team, so I had to forego the pleasure of seeing him play. We had to make the best of it for Tyler's sake.

One of the greatest losses for a child with a sibling who has autism is the loss of a normal brother or sister relationship. The sibling resists interaction on a normal level. For example, a child with autism might play in parallel (i.e., mimic the actions of other children) but not play interactively. At times, the child with autism does not even want siblings in the same room, much less touching the same toy. This is very hard for small children to comprehend; they long to play with a brother or sister who won't play with them.

I honestly don't recall any meaningful interactions between Terry and Taylor in the early and most difficult years of the disorder. Taylor was off in his own world, and it was hard for anyone else to break through for a long time. When Tyler and Taylor were very young, Tyler wanted to play cars with Taylor, while Taylor either just wanted to spin the wheels or tear them off the car and walk away. Tyler frequently asked, "Why won't he play with me?" I always tried to explain the oddities of autism, but it hurt to live in a house with a sibling who acted like he didn't want anyone near him. Our explanations of autism did not prevent hurt feelings. Children with autism have broken development, so those who love them have broken emotions. Tyler once asked if I was going to have any more babies, because he wanted to have a little brother who played with him.

Siblings of children with autism carry burdens and responsibilities that many people are not aware of. Safety is a looming, constant concern. The siblings of normal children are asked to help carry the diaper bag, but siblings of children with autism are often asked to guard the child from injuring himself. An extra set of eyes in the house can mean the difference between safety and stitches in the emergency room. "Where's Taylor?" is a constant question at our house.

I know my older children felt the strain of a brother who might hurt himself or simply wander off, unaware of the danger to himself. In those early years, I wore Taylor's safety like a heavy burden, and my other children must have felt it. I can't imagine what my edginess looked like. I remember Tyler's reaction when Taylor went missing while at his grandparents' house. I tried frantically to get the 911 operator to understand how dire the situation was. She seemed to be wasting time, repeating the same questions she had already asked. I finally yelled, "He's autistic! Get here now before he wanders onto the highway!" At that point, I saw Tyler's face. He looked more heartsick than I felt. I felt almost as bad for Tyler's suffering as I did for Taylor's potential danger. (That scary incident ended well: Taylor was discovered in a doorway at the rear of the high school by a young man who was part of the search party. He was safe and sound, perfectly oblivious to the panic his absence had caused. There was a brisk breeze in the air that day, and I've always said it was a fleet of angels hovering around Taylor until he was found.)

> *For He shall give His angels charge over you,*
> *To keep you in all your ways.*
> —*Psalm 91:11*

As mentioned in a previous chapter, Taylor had obsessive compulsions that almost drove us all to despair. Although the natural treatments have dramatically reduced Taylor's obsessive-compulsive disorder (OCD), Taylor still has it to a certain degree. In addition to the obsessions with dust and cracks, Taylor has always been obsessed with electronics. At times, we locked VCR and DVD players in closets on a high shelf and brought them down only when Taylor's OCD seemed to be under control. Currently, Taylor has his own set of electronics. But should the obsessions turn destructive again, the electronic devices will be hidden. So our other children have grown up with locks on their bedroom doors to keep Taylor from entering and destroying their things. (I can't tell you how many times one of the boys has exited a bedroom and shut the door with their keys locked inside.) When their friends come to visit, they sometimes laugh because my other sons lock their doors even when they come eat to supper. At times we say this is "the Gosney compound, going on lockdown." There's really nothing funny about it, but an occasional wisecrack helps to break the tension.

Taylor's television obsessions have occasionally been strong. Sometimes, he wanted all the television sets in the house to be on, tuned to the same show. (I wondered if he couldn't stand hearing the sounds of different shows because he had trouble filtering out conflicting noises.) At other times, he has been obsessed with tuning to specific channels simply because he wanted to see a particular logo in the bottom of the screen at all times. (Currently, he is most loyal to the NBC logo. He even hunts for it in newspaper ads and stares at it for long periods of time.) Logos and brand names are a common obsession for children with autism. Others in the house have shows they would like to watch, but Taylor is obsessively stuck on his preference. It's a battle to get an autistic mind to bend to another person's choice, especially when we have no clue what is driving that strong preference. There are times when we do get Taylor to give in, but many times, our son Tyler goes off to watch his show in his room alone. We never know from day to day if the television obsessions will be workable or not.

Taylor has had music obsessions that drove us all crazy. I am able to tune this out and not be as bothered by it, but others in the house are not. It is not unusual for Taylor to like a specific song on a CD for its strong beat, so he will replay that song for hours on end, sometimes for weeks in a row. He rocks to the beat of the song and is perfectly happy, gaining a sense of therapy from the rocking. But Tyler has said he goes to school and hears the lyrics of that song all day, like a drum beating in his head. If the song is one that Tyler liked before Taylor, then Tyler will definitely not like it by the time Taylor wears it out. Recently, when Terry and his wife Stephanie were home for a visit, Taylor played the same song the entire weekend. The next time Terry came home, he asked where that CD was. I think he was tempted to throw it away!

Autism has a way of eliminating certain activities from family life. One of our deepest losses as a family has been the ability to travel. My husband and I both have fond memories of family vacations we went on as children, but our own children have never been on any kind of family trip or vacation. Taylor's autism has confined us at home because some of his behaviors would make such a trip impossible or so exhausting that it would not be refreshing for anyone. Not long after my son Terry was married, Terry and his bride Stephanie took Tyler on a vacation with them. They could have easily gone alone, but instead they decided to treat Tyler to the trip as well. Sometimes, God uses those in your own family to paint a picture of healing and caring for each other.

You might read this chapter and believe the siblings would have trouble loving the brother or sister with autism, but quite the opposite is true. Our sons Terry and Tyler love Taylor deeply, and it is quite evident. Even though children with autism cause disruption and much sacrifice in the home, their siblings love them in spite of all the problems. The siblings might have to deal with some difficult emotions as they grow up, but the love will still be there. They grow up to realize that love is what a family is all about and to understand why their parents did what they did. As an adult, Terry is intrigued with the topic of autism and reads articles he finds on the Internet while surfing. Every time the child with autism has an accomplishment or overcomes a difficult hurdle in life, the siblings will be among the first to rejoice and tell others, as is the case in my family. I think Terry and Tyler rejoiced as much as my husband and I when Taylor's nutrient therapy began to show benefits. They needed to see a move of God as much as we did.

The heartache and abnormality of autism can also cause siblings to be very mature for their age. I believe the siblings of children with autism have to grow up a bit faster; as a consequence, they tend to think more deeply than most kids their age. Growing up with disability in their family, they learn what life is really about. They also come to appreciate things that children in normal families take for granted. Siblings are often fiercely protective of the child with autism and will defend that child if someone makes disparaging remarks about him or her. Sometimes siblings will also be hurt by kids making fun of other people who are handicapped, simply because they have a brother or sister who is also handicapped. That form of ridicule hits too close to home, and they do not like it at all.

As many losses and heartaches as my sons have endured, I believe they will be blessed with far more in the future. I also believe they will be young men who will be unable to ignore the pain and suffering in the lives of those around them. This alone will make them more available for whatever service God calls them to. They will have a sense of the human condition that other people might miss. I've chosen to hand their pain back to the Lord to be recycled for his glory. Even before they were old enough to understand what I meant, I told Terry and Tyler that God would give back what autism has stolen from our family and that he would use that gift for eternal purposes. I still believe that. A passage from the book of Joel eloquently describes the kind of restoration that God has promised my sons:

Be glad then, you children of Zion,
And rejoice in the LORD your God;
For He has given you the former rain faithfully,
And He will cause the rain to come down for you—

> *The former rain,*
> *And the latter rain in the first month.*
> *The threshing floors shall be full of wheat,*
> *And the vats shall overflow with new wine and oil.*
> *" So I will restore to you the years that the swarming locust has eaten,*
> *The crawling locust,*
> *The consuming locust,*
> *And the chewing locust,*
> *My great army which I sent among you.*
> *You shall eat in plenty and be satisfied,*
> *And praise the name of the LORD your God,*
> *Who has dealt wondrously with you;*
> *And My people shall never be put to shame.*
> *Then you shall know that I am in the midst of Israel:*
> *I am the LORD your God*
> *And there is no other.*
> *My people shall never be put to shame.*
> *—Joel 2:23–27*

May God bless Terry, Tyler, and all the siblings of children with autism. May their heartaches become golden in the Father's hands.

Ministering to the Siblings

Perhaps you feel drawn to help the siblings of children with autism and feel your service to the family should focus on them. Do not apologize. I believe God will call some people to help the child with autism and call others to focus on the siblings. It is God's way of taking care of everyone involved.

Reaching Out to the Siblings

If possible, invite the siblings to your home to get a break from dealing with the autism. They need a break as badly as the parents—sometimes more so. Perhaps you could have a standing day of the week when you will pick them up for a few hours. This could be something the siblings anticipate each week as their special time with you. If you have children who are about the same age as these children, that would be great. But if not, don't let this stop you from reaching out to them. Perhaps you could take them to your home for a visit or drive them on errands they need to run. If the children of the family are far apart in ages, you could take one child who is close to your children's age and another family could take the other sibling. Just be sure that no one is left out. You could also make your home available to the family of a child with autism when a crisis happens and they need a place to take their other children quickly. If the child with autism needs medical attention, it is much easier when places to stay have been lined up for the other children than it is to take the whole family to the hospital.

Ask Them About Their Lives

Many siblings of children with autism could use professional therapy to help them discuss their feelings, but many do not get it. They will value having a few people to whom they can open up, and this can keep them from breaking emotionally. Their parents may be so strained with the autism that the siblings feel guilty sharing their emotions with them for fear that their feelings will add more burden to their parents. Your support could be a form of therapy for the child.

The siblings of a child with autism may open up in stages, over time, as they become more comfortable with you. The first few times you ask about their life at home, they may not say much, but don't give up. Continue to ask how they are doing. They will eventually tell you about the issues on their hearts, and they will come to know you as someone who is genuinely concerned.

Bear one another's burdens, and so fulfill the law of Christ.
—Galatians 6:2

Acknowledge in Small Ways That Their Lives Are Broken Too

Sometimes the siblings get the sense that nobody has a clue how abnormal their lives are. While this may not be the case in your congregation and many people may, in fact, know, it is healing just to remind them that you understand the strain they are living under. Nobody can fix other people's problems entirely, but simple acknowledgement of the problem goes a long way toward helping the siblings cope. Share a word or two of encouragement before church services start or drop a card in the mail. Your words don't have to be fancy or full of wisdom; simply acknowledge that life at home isn't easy.

Keep Track of Their Accomplishments

As much as the siblings might need to discuss their feelings about autism, they also desperately need to talk about their own lives outside the home. If they have an area of giftedness or interest (e.g., sports, music, art), notice their accomplishments and let them know you are proud of them. It's a relief to know they can just be themselves in another setting and have something else to talk about.

Invite the Siblings When You Go on Short Trips

At different times my sons have been invited by people to go on weekend trips or to out-of-town ball games with their families. Occasionally, my own parents took them on trips, but others have done the same. While this is not the same as a family vacation by any means, it does allow the siblings to see some places and enjoy some experiences they would not otherwise have if their family is unable to go on vacations. If you can't afford to do this yourself, let the parents know ahead of time what you are considering and see if they can share the expense. Many times, the parents of a child with autism will jump at the chance to offer the siblings a break.

Pray for the Siblings and Let Them Know You Are Praying

Often, the siblings of a child with autism need as much prayer as anyone in the household, sometimes more. They bear pain just like the child suffering with autism, but in a different way. Many losses entered their world the day their sibling developed autism. It will encourage them spiritually to know that others are praying for them. A few of our Christian friends and family pray regularly for our other children. No matter how desperate the prayer requests become for Taylor, they always have Tyler and Terry on their minds as well.

I believe these farewell words from the apostle Paul sum up the theme of this chapter quite well:

And let our people also learn to maintain good works, to meet urgent needs, that
they may not be unfruitful. All who are with me greet you. Greet those who love
us in the faith. Grace be with you all. Amen.
—Titus 3:14–15

CHAPTER 5
Autism's Effect on the Extended Family

Just ask any member in the extended family of a child with autism whether autism has affected them. The answer will be a resounding yes! Most grandparents speak with a lump in their throats when they share the heartache of what it means for their grandchild to have autism. No parent ever dreams of autism landing in their family; nor does any grandparent, aunt, uncle, or cousin. The majority of grandparents today never knew what autism was until the past decade, when it suddenly rose to epidemic proportions and became a topic of discussion for talk shows and magazine articles. Now *autism* is a word they wish they only knew from news reports. It becomes far too real when it's in the next generation of your own family.

Many parents of children with autism share that they walk in a lifestyle of sheer grace and that only grace carries them from sun up to sundown. But it takes a different kind of grace to be a member of the extended family of a child with autism. They live in what I like to call "grace for the sidelines," the grace to be able to watch the pain in the lives of their family members. It's not the same heartache as dealing with autism in your own child, but it's very hard to swallow. The extended family members have to watch as the hopes and dreams of their own family members are shattered at the moment of the diagnosis and then watch as a life of hardship and trials unfolds. They might feel the need to keep a stiff upper lip and be strong for the family, but the hearts of grandparents and other extended family members still break in two.

Grandparents of children with autism feel obliged to do much more to help the family than they anticipated. They will have to step up and supply a helping hand where no other help is available. We call grandparents on both sides of our family all the time. They come to watch our son with autism and drive to pick up his siblings from events when we cannot go. We and many other families of children with autism call on grandparents to help with housework. The grandfathers on both sides of our family are called frequently to help with household repairs and other tasks. My husband and I shudder to think what we would have done over the years without the assistance they've provided us, often at a moment's notice. The grandparents of children with autism do much more than most people realize. One young mother recently told me that if her mother-in-law had not offered to watch her son with autism after school, she would not have been able to go back to work. She couldn't have found a sitter who knew her son well enough to watch him every day.

Many grandparents lay in bed at night praying for the futures of their grandchildren. But a grandchild with autism breaks their hearts to the point of desperation. That child is not more important than the other grandchildren, but he or she is starting life broken. It's just not in the natural scheme of life to begin with a hurdle as big as autism. My husband's mother, Mary Gosney, says, "It is so hard to see Taylor frustrated when he can't communicate. I pray for all my grandchildren, but Taylor's name is always first on my prayer list." While the heartache touches grandparents in ways that break their hearts, it can also teach them spiritual lessons that they never could have imagined. Although my family has talked openly from time to time about what it was like for them to watch Taylor's autism worsening, it wasn't until I asked my mother to put down her feelings that I realized the gravity of what my parents and other grandparents of children with autism must endure. Here's what my mother, Marilyn Hammock, had to say:

> What we as grandparents experience with an autistic grandchild is hard to put on paper. In what we call "The Dark Days of Autism," we felt so helpless. We wanted so badly to help but did not really know what to do. The worst days were when the OCD [obsessive-compulsive disorder] was in full swing. Taylor's obsessions with cracks, crevices, and liquids was almost unbearable. He poured liquid detergent along baseboards and often tipped over

furniture in order to get to the cracks along the baseboards. Their home was literally a shambles.

I would say the worst part was watching my daughter and her family's life turned upside down, always watching, always wondering what Taylor was doing or how he would react to things. But the bright side is watching Taylor progress in new and amazing ways. He is now able to communicate by writing down his thoughts, feelings, and desires. It's the victory we dreamed of for years when we did not know quite what we were praying for. Taylor's improvement is a 1,000%!

As a grandparent, I am also saddened by the responses I have heard several times when people hear of the strains of autism on a family. Some people have remarked, "What a burden!" To that, I reply, "No, what a blessing!" As Christians we believe God is sovereign and in control. We also believe that all that comes to us passes through his hands. To God be the glory!

Sometimes the concerns of grandparents seem to lessen as things improve, but sometimes they just change into new ones. I've befriended a grandmother named Gerrie, who has a grandson named Nick who has autism. Nick is older now and moving into the adult years. Gerrie says that even though Nick is older, he is still very affectionate toward her and her husband. Nick has graduated from high school and is trying hard to get a job, but his impaired speech hinders the process. So many parts of Nick's life are "grown up," so he desires an adult lifestyle, but he cannot understand why his autism gets in the way. Gerrie summed it up this way:

The older he gets, the greater the problems seem to be. He is so near normal, but he still isn't normal. This is so hard for him to accept. He talks about getting a job, an apartment, and a wife, yet he has never had a date. God bless his sweet heart.

Just as autism affects the child's family in their own homes, it can devastate extended family gatherings as well. The unpredictability and disturbances that afflict the child at home will be manifested in large family gatherings as well, sometimes even more so.

This is because the majority of children with autism like set schedules and predictability. They want things to stay the same on a daily basis. For this reason, many of these kids don't enjoy holidays in the same way typical children do.

Holidays and other special occasions often bring families together at grandparents' homes. Although children with autism may usually be affectionate and subdued with the grandparents, they can act out during special gatherings simply because they don't like all the hoopla and sensory disturbances. Christmas can be bothersome to a child with autism, not only for the break in routine, but because it brings the stimuli of Christmas lights, holiday fragrances, and furniture rearranged for decorating, not to mention holiday events to attend. Christmas is a sensory nightmare for a child with autism, especially in the early years before they learn coping skills.

As the mother of a child with autism, I used to dread Christmas because it was so unpredictable and hard to get through. Taylor seemed so overwhelmed and had a short fuse in terms of how much overload he could take. We often left these family gatherings early and could feel the sadness being shared by the rest of our family. As I was whisking Taylor out the door, I would see the pain in the eyes of my family. However, I knew not to look too long into their eyes. If I saw that their pain matched my own, I might fall apart. My mother-in-law, Mary Gosney, echoed my thoughts on the holiday losses with this comment:

> We have a large family and extended family. Holidays, birthdays, and family reunions have always been very important to us and especially to our son Bret. Bret has always been a family person who looked forward to family gatherings. It has been sad to see Taylor not enjoying the crowds and unable to handle the celebrations for very long. His mother, Sheila, usually has to forego the festivities and take Taylor home early. Sheila has missed so many occasions over the years.

Many times, I took Taylor home by myself so others in our family could stay and enjoy the occasion. But this made the situation seem even sadder. Sometimes Plan B is the only thing you can do, but it still hurts a great deal. My husband's parents enjoyed their fiftieth wedding anniversary with a lovely reception hosted by the family. Taylor became so unhappy that day that we had to leave early. In fact, he screamed much of the time he was there; he couldn't bear the noise and confusion. I know that not having all their children and grandchildren present that day was hard for my in-laws.

We are grateful that holidays have gotten so much better. They can still be unpredictable, but Taylor is much more at peace. We praise God for the nutritional treatment He led us to, treatment that we believe has helped Taylor in so many ways, including an improved ability to handle social gatherings and holidays.

Aunts and uncles are not removed from the pain. I know that our siblings on both sides of the family prayed for us often. I asked my brother, Terry Hammock, to give me a few words to describe what he felt over the years as he watched our lives unravel through Taylor's disability. Here's what he had to say:

> When my nephew Taylor was diagnosed with autism, we had no idea what it was. Very soon we realized that my sister Sheila, Bret, and the entire family were having their lives turned upside down. There was little normalcy to family life any longer.
>
> As much as they loved Taylor, he needed constant attention, and they began to live an exhaustive lifestyle of caring for and loving a child with autism. Family gatherings were sometimes quickly cut short. Many times, the Gosney family just could not do what other families could because of Taylor's needs. It broke my heart to see them so often exhausted and sometimes to the point where it seemed like they just could not go on. But by the grace of God, they did carry on and continue to love and care for Taylor. I believe that we all need to better understand the effects of autism on families and reach out and support these families with love and practical helps.

My husband's sister, Pam Drebes, is no stranger to heartache and disability. She herself is a blind amputee who has suffered from the ravages of diabetes, but she's said several times how she grieved for Taylor and felt helpless to know the heartache we were living with. Pam has never seen Taylor, but she loves him simply for the beauty of his being her nephew.

If you think autism is difficult for adults to grasp, just think what it must be like for other children in the extended family. It can be hard for them to figure out why their cousin acts the way he does, so they are not sure how they can relate to him. Over the years, young relatives have often asked me, "Why won't he talk to me?" Then I pull out my little memorized talk about Taylor's brain being broken. I try to let them know that messages coming into Taylor's ears are heard and understood, but he can't get messages back out of his mouth. I also try to get the child to look past Taylor's strange body movements and behaviors to see that he has very normal desires and thought processes underneath his autistic behaviors. I often tell them to keep saying hello to Taylor and just try to be his friend, even if he doesn't talk back.

As much as it baffles children at first, they do eventually understand Taylor's condition at some level. Sometimes I see them modifying games for Taylor's benefit. At other times, I see them trying to coax Taylor into playing a game, regardless of his autism. Often, Taylor lingers near the games they play, even though he doesn't fully interact with them. This is a great improvement from the days when he wanted nothing to do with his cousins.

As much as I think autism hurts the cousins and other children in the family, I firmly believe that it helps them spiritually, helping them learn how to love and care about a relative with a major disability. Our nieces and nephews are often burdened enough to pray for Taylor. I've heard of Taylor's being prayed for at other churches, and learned that the request was made by a niece or nephew. I have confidence that all of Taylor's cousins will spiritually benefit from growing up with his autism and learning how to relate to and love him through it. One of Taylor's cousins actually chose to make a career of teaching children with autism. You might say that Andrea, my husband's sister's daughter, has had more than the average share of inspiration. We pray that God uses Andrea greatly to help these broken children.

God sets the lonely in families.
—*Psalm 68:6a* NIV

While this chapter may be one of the shortest in this book, I feel that it may be one of the most enlightening for you. Most people see the serious needs of the immediate family touched by autism but don't think about the impact felt by the extended family. They have losses and needs as well, although they aren't nearly as great as the needs felt by the immediate family.

Ministering to the Extended Family

If you are connected to an extended family member of an autistic child, I've listed a few ministry ideas below.

Express Interest in Their Relative with Autism.

Do not assume that their nephew, niece, or grandchild is the same as another child with autism whom you know. Take the time to ask some questions to discover specifically how the child is affected by autism. Remain interested and contact them periodically to ask about the progress of the child.

Pray for the Child by Name.

Add the child to your prayer list. Pray faithfully for that child's needs, and let the extended family know you are praying. When special occasions come up on the calendar, pray for the success of that family's holiday events and let them know you are praying. Remember, the success of the child with autism at dealing with a holiday or gathering affects them too.

Clip Magazine or Newspaper Articles about Autism.

Clip any articles about autism that you see and send them to the extended family. This is a wonderful way to show their needs are important to you. If you hear of another child with autism being helped by a certain treatment, take note of the details and pass it along to the family. We never know how God will send us the information we need, and this is a great way to let the entire family know you are in tune and listening.

Our parents have had many articles clipped and handed to them at church by kind souls who are keeping an eye open for anything helpful. This simple act gives the grandparents an assurance that others truly care about their grandchild. The articles are always passed on to us, and we get the blessing as well.

Notify the Extended Family When Topics Dealing with Autism Are on Television.

Grandparents and other family members may not understand autism the way the immediate family does, and they are always looking for ways to learn more. Many times, the friends of grandparents on both sides of our family will call them with news of an upcoming television program on autism. Sometimes they call our house and let us know of the programs as well. It's just a simple way of letting the entire family know you care for them.

Situational Help for the Grandparents.

Find out as much as you can about the family's situation. Start by learning whether the grandmother or grandfather has been helping in a specific way, and then see if there's anything you can do to minister in that area. For example, you might discover that the grandmother comes over one day a week to clean house for the family. Or perhaps grandparents show up to babysit on certain days until the mother gets home from work. If this is the case, your gift of a home-cooked meal for the grandparents on that day would be a blessing. Or you might find out whether the grandfather is trying to help the family with particular chores or household improvements. If so, extra help could be enlisted for his physical efforts, which would speed the job up and show him that others care about his family too.

> *One generation passes away, and another generation comes;*
> *But the earth abides forever.*
> —*Ecclesiastes 1:4*

CHAPTER 6

Spiritual Encouragement for Families Affected by Autism

T here's no doubt about it: all parents need spiritual encouragement to raise their children. Parents of children with autism need a generous portion of spiritual encouragement on all fronts. It's difficult to raise a child who has continual setbacks, leaving parents and family exhausted emotionally, physically, and often spiritually. Even if the parents are Christians and have a good hold on the faith in their hearts, their faith will be tested in ways they never dreamed. They will need their friends' faith at times to lift them back up and remind them there is hope in Christ.

How can you spiritually encourage a family who is walking a journey so foreign to anything you've ever seen before? The answers are quite simple: by relying on God, his Word, and large doses of continual prayer. You do not need to understand the many facets of autism to encourage the parents of a child with autism to cling to the power of God. Your presence in their lives will go a long way toward keeping discouragement at bay. God's Word is unchanging and a faithful anchor for the soul. It never fails at what it is intended to do. When you have no words of your own wisdom or advice, don't worry: God's Word will pick up where your limited capabilities leave off.

> *So shall My word be that goes forth from My mouth;*
> *It shall not return to Me void,*
> *But it shall accomplish what I please,*
> *And it shall prosper in the thing for which I sent it.*
> —Isaiah 55:11

Spiritual encouragement has often come to me from people who probably didn't think about what they were going to say but who simply ran into me and allowed God to speak through them in the moment. Those people reminded me of things in God's Word in the most stressful years of Taylor's development when I didn't have two spare minutes to read the Bible. They had no idea their little tidbit reminders rang into my soul or that I would walk around whispering the verses they quoted as if they were fuel for my spiritual engine. Due to the stress, I couldn't digest much scripture or read for very long, but God knew I was hungry for Him like never before and needed His truth more than ever. If I received just a few powerful verses a week, I was set. Sometimes they were spoken to me; sometimes they arrived on a greeting card. But they always came when I needed them most and when my study time was the most limited. I was able to read the Bible more when Taylor entered school, but there were some years where I all I could do was to feed off the spiritual truth that was shared with me through the mouths and hearts of others. I recall several older ladies at church who clutched me tightly between services and quoted verses to me. Sometimes it was as simple as their telling me to remember that God will never leave us nor forsake us. When Monday rolled around and things were bad all over again, I heard, "God will never leave us nor forsake us," echoing in my head throughout the day.

The amount of spiritual encouragement you give to the family will also depend on where they are in their Christian walk. Were they new believers when their child was diagnosed with autism? If so, they will need far more spiritual encouragement than someone with years of Christian maturity under the belt. New believers may question God in different ways because they don't know God as well as someone who has more knowledge. Gear your spiritual encouragement for the level they need. Try not to judge them for any inappropriate reactions they have as they gauge their feelings against their faith. They may question God on one issue and then be totally at peace with it a few months later. If they begin to doubt God, pray, pray, pray.

There might be times when spiritual help is your primary act of service to the family of a child with autism, simply because their pain is too great to receive anything else. One season of the autism journey that will need much prayer and spiritual support is the actual time of diagnosis. At the onset of the diagnosis, the parents will grieve their child's autism in much the same way as a death. The diagnosis of autism means the death of the hopes and dreams the family held the day they brought their child home from the hospital. Grief actually comes in five stages: denial, anger, bargaining or reasoning with God, depression, and finally acceptance. Most parents travel through all five stages with autism. Each family is different and each person in the family may grieve differently. For example, a husband may enter quickly into the stages of grief, while the wife may begin her grieving at a later time and her stages of grief may last for different periods of time. I believe that I was so busy trying to help Taylor that I didn't grieve much at the onset of his diagnosis, but when we almost placed him in a mental-health facility, I definitely did. That devastating marker on the road of our journey triggered a physical and emotional depression, and I was stunned at how hard I fell. Christians would do well to be highly sensitive to the stages the parents are experiencing and then to pray accordingly and without judgment.

The family of a child with autism may need a great deal of prayer but crave the privacy to grieve in solitude. Others need people around them as they grieve. If the parents resist your efforts to physically help them at this time, do not be offended and don't give up. It's just an indication of a particular season of grief and how they want to walk through it. They will still be blessed by your tender offer to help. They might even call you back at a later date and take you up on your offer. In the meantime, pray continually and offer encouragement in other ways. Sending cards or scripture readings will let the family know you support them and respect their privacy to grieve. If you watch them, you will likely notice when their demeanor shifts and they are open to physical help again.

Some parents of children with autism report that grief or depression can be triggered by a time in the life of the child that would mark a normal milestone. For example, it can be painful to watch a neighbor's child go off to kindergarten while their child remains in a special-education environment. The parents may grieve when other teenagers obtain their driver's license because they know their child's autism will prevent that from happening. This much is certain: Grief is real, but so is God's ability to heal it. We live in a fragile world full of losses and disappointments. But we have a powerful Savior who died not only to save our souls but to offer us hope for this life. We who know him as Savior and Lord have access to this wellspring of hope that heals our brokenness.

> *Why are you cast down, O my soul?*
> *And why are you disquieted within me?*
> *Hope in God;*
> *For I shall yet praise Him,*
> *The help of my countenance and my God.*
> *Psalm 43:5*

While we as believers are action-oriented, we cannot ever underestimate the sheer power of prayer in any situation, including autism. Some of our family's greatest victories were the byproduct of answered prayers. One came on the night of Taylor's older brother Terry's wedding in February 2006. As their mother, I was concerned for everyone. I wanted Terry and Stephanie to have a beautiful wedding, but I longed to have Taylor present for the occasion. I chose to submit my desire to God. I asked a handful of Christian ladies to pray with me that Taylor would handle the festivities as long as possible so that we could have the memory of the presence of all of our kids at the reception. We just wanted our whole family together for one night. (This does not sound like a big deal to somebody with normal children, but for us this prayer request was gigantic.) I had no clue just what would happen or how God would respond, but I dared to ask God anyway. I even bought Taylor his own tuxedo as an act of faith that he would indeed be part of the family that day.

On the day of Terry's and Stephanie's wedding, Taylor stayed with Sara, his respite worker, until the ceremony ended. It was her job to get him to the church for photos and accompany him to the reception to help us tend to him. Sara was actually my caretaker that day, along with my friends who were at their homes praying about this.

At the reception, a vision of answered prayer unfolded before our eyes. Taylor went out onto the dance floor and danced the entire night. He acted like he truly wanted to be there. He sat in his chair when asked. He ate dinner with our guests and literally left us in awe of his behavior. There were only flickers of unruly behavior that caused concern. Numerous people who knew that Taylor was autistic stopped me and asked where he learned to dance. Many people just stood and watched him in amazement. (A few of his dance moves caused us to laugh until tears filled our eyes.) That was one of the most precious answers to prayer we've ever enjoyed. It had all the earmarks of the One who made Taylor and was still in charge of his life. As Taylor danced that night, my soul danced with delight and praise before the Lord.

> *You have turned for me my mourning into dancing;*
> *You have put off my sackcloth and clothed me with gladness,*
> *To the end that my glory may sing praise to You and not be silent.*
> *O Lord my God, I will give thanks to You forever.*
> —Psalm 30:11–12

Spiritual help is by far the most important thing you can offer the family of a child with autism. This is something every believer can do for the family. There may be times you can help the family in physical ways and other times when you can only pray. Never underestimate the times when praying is all you can do. Sometimes I think God allows such situations to make us realize how badly we need His power. So many Christians in our community have prayed for us that I joke that everyone knows us before we know them. One day I walked into a florist shop to place an order and had Taylor with me. When I spoke my name, a sweet Christian lady looked around the counter and said she and her church had prayed for Taylor for years, so she recognized our names. She said she wanted to see what Taylor looked like. It's our belief that every day, even on every bad day we've endured at our house, the Holy Spirit was calling on a prayer warrior to lift us up.

I've often said that our finding the new doctors who helped our son so much wasn't the result of our searching. It resulted from years of prayer, like a giant wall that our family and everyone else was building on our behalf. Every prayer was a brick on the wall, building higher toward God's face. One day the wall reached a certain height, and God's perfect will unfolded with the right answer at the right time.

Never stop praying for the family of a child with autism, even when answers do not appear on the horizon. You are building a wall of prayer for the child and the family, and one day the Lord will answer with his perfect will. By then, you will have prayed so much that it will be your victory as well.

Ministering Spiritually to the Family

Remind Them of the Word When You Are in the Word

When you read God's Word and find encouraging passages, take the time to write them down for the family. They could be written by hand on a note card, printed from your computer, or reproduced by any other method you can think of. Give these passages to the family, either by hand when you see them at church or in the mail. You could even e-mail passages to them if they are online and use e-mail. Tell them how God ministered to you through these verses as you read them.

Remember, you are spoon-feeding them until they are able to come to the table of God's Word again. They are still starving for truth, but their present situation consumes any time they once had for Bible study. If they are new believers or unfamiliar with the things of God, this might be the most sensitive and powerful ministry you can offer them.

Keep Their Names Permanently on Your Church Prayer Chain

Autism can wear the family out. The many changes and discouragements that arise can make the family feel they are tiring others by reciting the details. Last week's victory can become this week's defeat.

I suggest that you make your church's prayer-chain coordinator aware of the family and have the coordinator contact the family on a regular basis, perhaps every two or three weeks, to see what prayer needs the family has. This will let the family know that they don't have to call repeatedly to post their own updates and that others care enough to call them. Keeping your church updated on the family will also make busy people aware of the family's ministry needs, which increase if the situation worsens. If a regular prayer update indicates an urgent need, then people will be moved to action, more than if they heard nothing.

Have Smaller Groups Adopt the Family in Prayer

Our church has various prayer ministries, but one in particular is a humble group of ladies who meet for prayer every Tuesday. Most of these women are elderly, unable to serve in the physical ways they once could. But they can still pray, and they do it very well. I can't count how many times these tenderhearted women have stopped me and asked for updates on Taylor over the years. Often, I've had nothing good to report, but they've kept on praying. They have never stopped praying. (I've been told it's very hard to get off their prayer list. Their motto is, "There are only three ways to get us to stop praying: get saved, get well, or die.")

> *Rejoice always, pray without ceasing, in everything give thanks;*
> *for this is the will of God in Christ Jesus for you.*
> *—1 Thessalonians 5:16-18*

Teach Your Children to Pray

Young children may have plenty of questions about a friend or relative with autism, such as what the problem is and why he or she acts so oddly. Be honest with them. Tell them in children's terms what it means to have autism. If you lack the ability to do that, by all means ask the parents of the child with autism for an explanation they feel would be understood by your children. Then ask your children to adopt certain needs of that family in prayer. For example, have one child pray specifically for the dietary concerns, concerns specific enough for a child to understand and pray about. Have your children periodically remind the family that they are praying for that particular need in their child's life.

Ask the parents for a photo of the child with autism; your children can put it on the refrigerator or in their rooms to remind them to pray. This is a wonderful way to teach children to pray for things they might not fully understand. In addition, it builds compassion into young hearts that will grow into a lifetime of love for the handicapped.

Praying God's Word on Behalf of the Family

Praying God's Word is a practice that may already be familiar to you. It takes passages of Scripture and prays them to the Father, inserting specific people's names or situations into the passages. One friend of mine said she loves doing it because it's speaking God's own language back to him in prayer. I've found it very healing at times to practice this simple act of faith.

If you've never prayed God's Word, take hold of some promises from God's Word and combine them with prayer. Another way to bless the family spiritually when you pray God's Word is to write the passage down for the family and give it to them. (If you do this, I recommend that you give them both the original passage from the Bible and the customized prayer for them using the passage.) A few examples of using God's Word as a prayer are given below.

Scripture

"For I know the plans I have for you," declares the Lord, "plans to prosper you and not to harm you, plans to give you hope and a future."
—Jeremiah 29:11 NIV

Prayer Using the Passage

Lord, I know that You have plans for Taylor and I know You are a good and righteous God. Your plans for Taylor include goodness, and You plan to prosper and not harm Taylor. We know You have a hope and future for Taylor as well, and we ask for healing in accordance with Your good plan. In Jesus' name, amen.

Scripture

Yet in all these things we are more than conquerors through Him who loved us. For I am persuaded that neither death nor life, nor angels nor principalities nor powers, nor things present nor things to come, nor height nor depth, nor any other created thing, shall be able to separate us from the love of God which is in Christ Jesus our Lord.
—Romans 8:37–39

Prayer Using the Passage

Dear heavenly Father, I know we are more than conquerors through You because of Your love for us. And I am persuaded that You love Taylor and that there is nothing that exists to separate Taylor from your love; not life, death, angels, principalities, or powers. Taylor isn't even separated by the things of the present or anything that comes. Height nor depth or any other thing cannot possibly separate Taylor from Your love either. Even autism can't separate Taylor from Your matchless love. All of this solid and unchanging love is made possible through the death and resurrection of Christ Jesus our Lord and the very maker of Taylor's entire body. And that, dear Father, is why I bring Taylor before You today. In your love and mercy, amen

Simple Gifts That Stir the Soul to Worship

All of us are created to worship God, and worship is crucial to surviving any crisis. Our feelings of helplessness are laid aside when we stand before the holiness of God and realize the wonder of who he really is. So you can provide an important form of spiritual support for families of children with autism by helping them to worship.

Several kind sisters in Christ gave me worship music at my lowest hour. Sometimes they bought a CD for themselves, were transformed by the words, and decided to give me one too. I've stood in my house with hot tears rolling down my face, full of the glory of God in the moment. Even the stress of autism can't overpower the presence of God, for he stands supreme over everything. I had already known worship was a powerful restorative experience; but after our son's struggle with autism, I realized even more its healing power for my personal brokenness.

Keep your eyes open to any gift that you think will benefit the family and remind them of the eternal God who still loves them. It could be a devotional book, wall plaque, or worship music. This particular act of ministry could be helpful for any member of the family—the parents or siblings, even the child with autism.

As iron sharpens iron,
So a man sharpens the countenance of his friend.
—*Proverbs 27:17*

Bible Study for Desperate Times

Invite the parents of children with autism to attend any Bible studies your church may be sponsoring. Even if they can't come, they will appreciate being invited. If they clearly want to come to the study groups, see if you can create a way to help make it possible. For example, if the mother cannot attend the study, you could attend on her behalf and then meet privately with her to watch the videos or discuss the week's study. If both parents want to take the study together, offer to circulate the videos or other study materials to them. If possible, offer to watch their child at the church while they attend the Bible study meetings.

Host a Prayer Meeting on Their Behalf

We host fund-raisers, auctions, and other events to benefit the terminally ill. Why not host a prayer meeting for a family dealing with autism? I believe any parent would be speechless to know their church met to pray for the healing of their family and their child with autism. The parents may or may not be able to attend. Even if they cannot, they will be touched to know others are meeting together for corporate prayer on their behalf. Specific prayer concerns could be gathered from the family prior to the meeting to give people a sense of their most pressing needs.

Is anyone among you sick? Let him call for the elders of the church, and let them pray over him, anointing him with oil in the name of the Lord. And the prayer of faith will save the sick, and the Lord will raise him up.
—James 5:14–15a

CHAPTER 7

How Autism Affects Family Finances

Autism can wreak havoc on a family's finances. Often, the family has no clue what the diagnosis will mean to the different aspects of the family life, but it doesn't take too many years to discover the truth. Not all cases of autism are the same and not all family financial situations will be the same. However, autism introduces some financial constraints that affect every family. For example, many mothers of children with autism realize that they cannot work outside the home and also provide the necessary parental care. They often have a difficult time finding a babysitter who can handle their child's autism.

Occasionally, these mothers are still able to hold down a job, but most families of children with autism suffer financially. Consider the extra expense that treatments for autism bring to the family. We used the same type of doctor for years for Taylor's medical care. Those doctors prescribed medications that insurance paid for. But when Taylor's life fell apart and prescription drugs failed us, we began searching for alternatives. We turned to doctors who used all-natural treatments for Taylor's autism. These treatments have been far more effective in Taylor's situation, but the expense of these natural treatments has never been covered by our medical insurance. We can spend anywhere from $150 to $200 per month on natural supplements, and this is pretty typical for families using this approach. The Food and Drug Administration cannot verify the medicinal value of these nutrients as it can with pharmaceutical drugs, so the majority of insurance companies will not offer reimbursement. I've often said that if insurers only knew that these methods create healthier children and reduce medical costs in the long run, perhaps they would get on the bandwagon and pay for them. But that's a problem I cannot solve alone.

Many parents of children with autism try alternative therapies for their children's autism. New theories and treatments are announced in medical articles on a frequent basis, and parents are often eager to find something new to try. While nutrient therapy is gaining popularity, other families try specialized diets to answer the child's needs. These include the Feingold Diet and the gluten-free and casein-free diet, also known as the GFCF diet.

The Feingold Diet attempts to establish a pattern of more natural eating and eliminates four categories of food additives: artificial flavoring, artificial coloring, artificial sweetener, and several artificial preservatives. This diet can greatly reduce hyperactivity and is implemented in stages to help parents discover the greatest offenders in the child's diet. This diet is useful for numerous disorders other than autism.

The GFCF diet offers other benefits for some children with autism. Gluten is the protein found in wheat and several other grains. Casein is the protein found in cow's milk. Not only are gluten and casein found in bread and dairy products, but they are frequently found as ingredients in many other food products on the market, from seasoning packets for chili soup to natural flavorings in chocolate chips. A gluten-free, casein-free diet is one of the costliest approaches to treating autism. A small box of gluten-free saltine-type crackers can sell for over four dollars, and not many retail stores have them. Many parents resort to mail order, which costs them even more. Substitute dairy items can be purchased as well, but they are much higher in price than their regular dairy counterparts. This diet is helpful for some children with autism who lack certain body chemicals to break down these two proteins. When they ingest gluten or casein, their bodies produce a peptide, which enters the bloodstream and either causes the autism symptoms or greatly exacerbates them. Excluding these from the diet can reduce or eliminate certain symptoms. Some families say the change in their children with autism is miraculous when using this diet. To implement the GFCF diet, many parents will forego purchasing prepared foods and prepare meals from scratch. Everything from new flours to better kitchen equipment will be needed to accomplish this.

All special diets add some expense to the family budget. Abstaining from entire groups of food or buying specialty products means a family cannot shop for items on a weekly sale; they must shop for food based on their child's need. In addition to being expensive, special diets can be very time-consuming for the parents. But we are willing to do anything we can to help our kids—no matter the time, sacrifice, or expense. Our family tried the GFCF diet several years ago but didn't find that it helped Taylor very much. We did learn a great deal, though. (We discovered exactly how bagels and other breads are made—and it's a whole lot of work!) It wasn't the first specialty diet we tried, and it likely won't be the last.

Autism can affect the family's budget in other ways. Our son's autism caused a lack of coordination. Combined with his curious and obsessive nature, his clumsiness caused him to break things all the time. We are constantly replacing things that other families would use for years before ever replacing. Our CD players have been replaced two to three times a year, and Taylor has broken things much more valuable than that. Sometimes his obsession with the buttons on an electronic gadget will prompt him to push them in an inappropriate manner, which eventually breaks the device. (One reason he does this is because he loves to hear static, and pushing various buttons at the same time will create that noise, as well as breaking the item at the same time.) Leaving Taylor unattended with an item for just a minute can result in having it broken. Taylor's strong desire for electronics has left us doing without camcorders, digital cameras, or other expensive items simply because he breaks them faster than our budget will allow us to replace them. In speaking to other parents of children with autism, some have told me similar stories of inadvertently destructive behavior.

Children with autism can have obsessions with food, toys, and just about anything you can name. Obsessions mean extra expense. We've tried hard to work with some of Taylor's obsessions. For example, if a toy that keeps him busy for hours on end happens to break, we will try to replace that toy quickly, even if it means we don't have money for something else. Food obsessions are often quite expensive. In the early years of Taylor's autism, he ate chicken patties every single day with tons of ketchup, often eating as many as six patties a day. This continued for years. When he finally stopped eating chicken patties, we were shocked. Although Taylor has gotten less obsessive in this regard, we have still been known to dart off quickly to the store for a food that is his current favorite. He may eat a favorite food for weeks in a row before getting tired of it or tolerating something different. (My husband often heard, "Honey, can you run to the store? Taylor is out of bacon." That meant he needed to put his shoes on and head out to the store, regardless of the hour.)

The strains on our budget have been difficult, but they have taught us that God will either supply extra resources or teach us new and creative ways to make do. My husband says that at times it has been almost comical to watch God teach us how to rely on him for everything, including the very basics of life. Only until after the high cost of autism grabbed our pocketbooks did we learn the art of clipping coupons and how to combine them with sale prices. We often walk out of stores with many items in our carts that are free or almost free. Clerks at the register say, "Now how did you do that?" We've come to realize that God chooses to manifest himself to his children even in grocery stores.

Many times we have had more bills at the end of the month than money. We've been blessed on numerous occasions with monetary gifts from both sides of our family; and we've had relatives volunteer to pay bills for us to help ease financial tension in the budget. At other times, people outside our family (even outside our church) have felt led to help. Each gift taught us to be humble and grateful, and caused us to look up to the Lord as our true provider.

Not everyone is able to give financial help to a family dealing with autism, but if you think this is an area where God is calling you to help, he will make that clear. Sometimes a good relationship already exists between you and the family of a child with autism, so giving a financial gift doesn't seem complicated. But some people would feel uncomfortable just handing a check or cash to a family in need, or they fear the recipients will be uncomfortable. These questions may keep people from reaching out in a financial way. But just as there are different ways to physically help these families, there are different ways to help financially. If the money is presented as a gift, with a loving spirit, it will likely be received with gratitude.

Ministering Financially to the Family

Many ideas for financial gifts spring to mind in this situation. These are just a few suggestions to get you thinking:

Anonymous Giving to the Family

If you feel led to give money to the family of a child with autism but would like to keep it anonymous, there are a few ways to do this. Most churches will be happy to pass a financial gift along to a family in need while keeping the donor's identity confidential. Money can be given to the church and designated for this purpose, to be rerouted through the treasurer or church secretary. The church can simply notify the family that an anonymous gift has been sent to them via the church. Another way is to donate money to the family through their closest, most trusted relatives. The family would be blessed by knowing someone is reaching out to their loved ones and will keep the secret if asked.

Use the Child's Birthday as a Special Time to Give

If you desire to give something toward the general expenses of the child's care, the child's birthday is a great opportunity to place some money in a greeting card and give it to the parents. Write something personal in the card, saying that to celebrate the life of their child you would like to contribute toward the child's medical treatment or daily expenses.

Giving Toward a Special Need the Child Has

Perhaps you hear that a child with autism needs something new, such as a bed, new car seat, or swing set. This could be a great opportunity to give. Place some money in a card with a heartfelt note to the parents, saying something like, "We truly love your family and would love to give toward the new bed for your daughter."

Paying Toward Medical Services

After getting to know the family, feel free to ask about the child's medical care and what treatments the child receives. If you learn the doctor's or clinic's name, this will help you in gift giving. Do they have insurance that pays for only part of the treatment? You could pay money directly to their account at the doctor's office, toward the part of the expense that insurance won't pick up. If you choose to do this anonymously, make sure you get a receipt; then have a trusted relative or friend let you know if the family was properly credited. Anonymous giving may not be possible in this case. If so, send the family a card with the doctor's receipt for your gift. Let them know how much you love their family and how God led you to help in this special way. They will arrive for their next doctor's visit feeling like God went ahead of them and provided for their needs.

And my God shall supply all your need according to His riches in glory by Christ Jesus. Now to our God and Father be glory forever and ever. Amen.
—Philippians 4:19–20

Sponsor a Month of Treatment

Perhaps God is calling you to lighten the family's budget strain by "sponsoring" a month of the child's treatment. If this amount is too high for you, perhaps you could find two or more families to make a joint gift.

If the child is taking natural treatments or other alternative therapy, a casual conversation with the parents will reveal the approximate amount they spend on it. Many people have asked us in passing how expensive our son's supplements are. I've never considered that a nosy question. Usually, someone will say something like, "Wow, that sounds expensive. Is that something insurance pays for?" And that conversation may lead to a gift. Such financial support brings a sense of relief to a tight budget, and it blesses the family to see that others desire to help. Place the money or check in a card and write a simple note telling them you feel led to sponsor the next month's treatments. It would also be appropriate to share a Scripture passage about healing.

A Blessing for Their Journey

Financial help for out-of-town medical trips is another great way to help. These trips usually entail hotel and other expenses. There are numerous ways to help the family with medical trips:

Ask ahead of time where they plan to stay and purchase a gift card for them in whatever amount you choose. If this isn't possible, simply send the family a check with a nice card saying you want to help with their hotel expense for their doctor visit.

Gift cards for gasoline are also appropriate. Numerous trips each year can drain a family, especially if the clinic is far away. A gift card for gasoline in any amount would lighten the expense and help the family. An easy choice would be to a gas station in your own town; they could fill up before they leave.

Gift cards for dining help cut costs on trips out of town. Find out which restaurants they normally eat at and purchase gift cards for those locations. Gift cards for many eateries can now be purchased online. Most families of children with autism tend to eat at the same places when they go out because the child will pick favorites and stick with them, no matter what. (We ate for so many years at McDonald's that I thought we should have bought stock in the company.)

A gift basket for the road might be highly appreciated. It could include a few small handheld items for the child with autism that would be fun and help occupy time. If the child has a handheld electronic game player that he or she enjoys, the addition of a new game cartridge may fascinate the child while in the car. Include some snacks or drinks for everyone. If the child uses a special diet, fresh fruit is usually a great choice. If in doubt, a quick call to the family, close friend, or grandparent will help you decide what to put in your gift box or basket.

> *But a generous man devises generous things,*
> *And by generosity he shall stand.*
> *—Isaiah 32:8*

Gift Certificates for Special Diets

If the child is using a special diet, this is another opportunity to make a gift. Ask the parents where they buy the majority of the special food needed; then surprise them with a gift certificate from that store or company. The next time they buy special food for their child, they will be reminded of how much you care. If you feel led to give toward dietary needs and cannot find the information needed to purchase a gift card, by all means give the family some money and state that you'd like for them to put it toward the extra dietary expenses. In the presentation of your gift, take a few moments to remind them that you believe they are great parents and you want to be a part of what they are doing to help their child's autism. Then your gift comes with the extra blessing of affirmation from someone else.

The Gift of Special Equipment for the Home

Many children with autism need therapy equipment for their homes. These items balance them and help them cope with the autism, especially when they are not at school to receive various therapies. Some families have plenty of help from social agencies that purchase these items, but some families get no agency help for different reasons.

If you discover that the family needs a piece of equipment for their child, this is a possible area of ministry. Larger groups of people might be able to pool their money to buy something like this. Adult Sunday school classes, youth groups, or other groups of people could pool their resources to obtain such an item for the family. They could gather a collection or do a group fundraiser, such as a yard sale, to purchase the therapy item. Creative ideas for raising the money are usually no problem, once the need is known.

Is There a Handyman in the House?

Most children with autism are accident-prone. Their unusual obsessions often combine with their accident-prone nature to break things much more quickly than in homes not dealing with autism. If you have men or women in your church family who are very handy at repairing things, their service to the family could be of great value. Find out who these people are. If you have people who can repair plumbing, electrical service, appliances, woodwork, automobiles, electronic devices, and so on, make a list of these individuals and approach them privately to see if they are willing or able to help.[2] Then present the list to the family and let them know you've spoken to these individuals. Explain that these repair people would like to make themselves available for future needs that arise in their household. Just knowing they are willing and able to help with repairs will be a financial blessing to the family, as well as encouraging them personally.

Relief with Basic Living Expenses

Any relief with basic living expenses will bless the family and loosen the budget.

God will lead you to what you can do in this regard, but let me give you a few examples to get you started:

If you have livestock processed and fill your freezer with meat each year, offer some to the family to ease their grocery expense. This is also true for any gardeners who have extra produce at harvest time. A few friends

---

2. If these individuals do repair work for a living or a side income, use special sensitivity as you approach them. Not everyone can afford to offer free services, but some may be able to offer their services at a discount instead. Simply ask and thank them for whatever they offer.

always bring my favorite fruits and vegetables to my door each summer. I've never had the time to plant a garden, so I consider this a great blessing.

Help with the family's utility bills. During a particularly difficult time, my husband sent me to City Hall to pay our utility bill. When I arrived, I was told someone had anonymously put a substantial amount of money into our account, leaving me with far less to pay at the counter. We never had a clue who the giver was, but that gift was a vivid answer to our prayers for provision. As I left City Hall that day, all I could think of was the biblical account of Abraham when he named the mountain "The-Lord-Will-Provide" after the miraculous provision he received.

Any time of year when families normally incur financial strain (e.g., Christmas, back-to-school) presents an opportunity for you to step forward with a gift to ease their financial pressures. Remember, anything you can give toward regular living expenses, anonymous or otherwise, will leave the family with more funds to help with the special needs of their household.

Spontaneous Gestures to Help Other Family Members

When you meet any financial need for any member of the family, you will save them money that will be a financial blessing. It need not even be a large dollar amount. On numerous occasions, people did something spontaneous to help one of my other children or another member of the family. I'm sure they acted because they knew it would help the finances in general. Concert tickets were bought, camp bills paid, and other spontaneous gestures of financial help received along the way. I am sure these kind souls just saw an opportunity to bless someone in our household, and they seized it. God knows who they are, and I am sure He will bless them in return.

Look for any way to bless the family of a child with autism and relieve their financial strain. If you are open and looking, the Lord will show you what he wants you to do.

We believe that all we have comes from God and we give it out of His hand
—1 Chronicles 29:14b, (Dutch paraphrase).[3]

---

3. Quoted from www.samaritanspurse.org/index.php/Who_We_Are/financial_ accountability/.

CHAPTER 8

How Should the Church Respond to Autism?

Many of the ministry ideas described so far in this book refer to individual or family responses to a family suffering with autism. However, what should the church's corporate response to autism be? Many churches today have no clue about how to respond to autism, mainly because they lack a basic understanding of the disorder.

Churches are known for going door-to-door to reach the lost, unchurched, or unloved in their communities. But sooner or later, a neighbor's front door will swing open and you will encounter the family of a child with autism. What will the church offer to accommodate and minister specifically to the issue of autism in those families? This epidemic of our generation begs for a response from the church.

For decades, many churches have sponsored ministries and special classes for adult individuals who are handicapped, but children with special needs often fall through the cracks. The needs of children with autism are even more specific. I've come to personally know many other parents of children with autism. Often they are Christians, but sometimes they are not. One common remark from these parents is that their church or other churches they've visited offer nothing to meet the personal needs of their child with autism. Unbelieving parents will seldom visit a church if they already know there is nothing there for their child dealing with autism. If they can't attend church as a family, they simply will not come. You can invite them all you want, but they will not come as a fractured family unit.

This need should be addressed because autism is an epidemic that is not expected to go away anytime soon.

Years ago, someone came up with the idea that parents needed a break from their children so they could be in church services to worship and listen without distractions. The idea of the church nursery was born. The same concept should apply to parents of children with autism, but the accommodations need to be entirely different.

What Should Churches Offer for the Child with Autism?

Depending on the level of impairment, a child with autism may fit fairly well in the church nursery up to a certain age, but from a certain point on, that will no longer work. These children cannot sit still or keep quiet for the length of a church service. For different reasons, these children need a place of their own, a safe haven they can actually look forward to visiting. This could be as simple as a room that is sensory-friendly, well-monitored, and has an adequate amount of appropriate things to do. The following are some suggestions for creating a sensory-friendly autism classroom:

Lighting

Artificial lighting is of utmost importance in a room for children with autism. Many of these children are sensitive to florescent lighting, so it should be avoided. Diffused lighting would be the best choice. Lights with a dimmer switch would also be beneficial. These children tend to be more light-sensitive on particular days, so the dimmer switch would allow adjustments to be made. Some children with autism prefer no overhead lights at all and may like a room with only natural lighting with the blinds open.

If electrical lighting malfunctions and creates flickering, this should be addressed promptly. This is also true if the lighting creates any noise, such as the low buzzing noise that some bulbs put off before they go bad. Check the lighting regularly to intercept any problems such as these.

Soundproof Room

The room need not be soundproof in the technical sense, but it should be far enough away from the sanctuary or other classrooms that there isn't much background noise. Overlapping noises can greatly upset some children with autism because they have trouble filtering out noises and can become overwhelmed. This will also help shield the worship services from any extra noise the children could make.

Calming Colors on the Walls

It's a well-known fact that colors affect our moods, and this is especially true of children dealing with autism. Strong, bright colors such as yellow or orange can adversely affect the child's mood. Softly colored walls without a great deal of busyness or posters are best for the room for these children. If another group needs to use the room, let them use one wall for things they need to hang and let the other walls remain clear of clutter.

A Variety of Furniture

The classroom should have typical furniture in it, such as tables and chairs that are the right size and height for the age of the children. The children will use them to do activities such as reading or coloring. It will create a station-like atmosphere similar to that of their school classrooms. If possible, it would be good to include some soft furniture as well. If the size of the room will accommodate it, a couch or recliner would be of great value to the children. Many children with autism rock repetitively to calm themselves, and they do so against soft furniture. For children who have tactile sensory issues, the furniture offers an alternative to help them cope on days when their sensory issues are more of a problem. Sometimes life with autism is so hard that the child just wants to lie down and not do anything. Having a couch would create a soft place where they can fall.

Appropriate and Interesting Activities

The parents' input would be of great value in supplying your room w activity items for children with autism. Music is a common favorite for children dealing with autism, so a CD player and stack of CDs is a g place to start. Some of these kids love music so much that they would l to a favorite CD the entire time that church is in session. Some chi with autism like certain board games. If the child is fond of a par cartoon, have at least one episode in the classroom that the child have at home. This will create a level of anticipation about going to Someone in your church likely has an older television they could to the classroom; you do not need anything fancy to play such v Handheld games are often popular, as are TV-based games. Ho caution when choosing games to prevent inappropriate material from being in your church building.

Have someone check any electronics in the classroom prior to church services to make sure they are in working order and have fresh batteries. If a favorite item isn't working and needs to be removed from the room, it is best to call the parents so they can warn the child. Any changes like this can upset the child a great deal, but he or she can usually cope much better if warned ahead of time that the item will be gone. Remember, these children depend on having things happen predictably, on cue, and they have trouble coping when things don't go according to script.

Add New Things Periodically

As you add new items to the autism classroom, keep standby favorites in the room. The parents can advise you about what items are needed if you are uncertain. Often, families in your church would like to have a place where they can donate toys and electronics that their own children are tired of. Let the families of your church know their unwanted items may be welcome as donations for the autism classroom.

Have Everything in Its Place and a Place for Everything

Children with autism crave order, especially in a classroom setting. For this reason, store the items they use in specific places in your closet or storage shelves. Mark a space for the CD player, CD container, markers, crayons, video games, and so on. Make little cards or labels with the name of each item and place each one on the shelf where each item goes. This simple act will give children with autism the mental peace they need and will also help them at clean-up time. They will likely put things away willingly if you take the time to label the space where they go.

Protect the Room from Disorder

It is critical that other church members understand how important the items in the autism classroom are to the children. If someone borrows a CD player and takes it to another room and then doesn't bring it back, the staff will have no idea where to look. This can ruin the success of the day for the child. This is not a case of a child who has bratty behavior but of a little mind that operates in a completely different way and has unusual needs for order and continuity. Put a well-written note on the cabinet or closet door where equipment and supplies are kept, explaining that such items should be borrowed only in an emergency and must be brought back promptly.

A Clock on the Wall
Autistic children love clocks and can tell time from a very early age, often before an adult teaches them what it means. They can watch a clock on the wall and know exactly when things are supposed to happen, so be sure to equip the autism classroom with a clock on the wall. Each child will come to know about how long your services run and will use the clock to help create order in his or her mind. If the child is having an off day and seems to be more anxious, the teacher can point to the clock and tell them about how much longer they have before their parents return. This will help them cope.

Alternative Activities
Children with autism and their attendants will need a breather or different surroundings on occasion. Going to another room for part of the time period will help break up the time and make it go faster. If you have a large room, such as a basement or a gym, that is accessible during church services, this can be used as an alternate activity. It could be as simple as taking a few items to the room to play with or playing a certain game each time you go. Some churches have play areas outside their building, which is also a good option.

Depending on the children's abilities, they may be able to attend a small portion of the regular church service, especially if they are fond of music. When the music is over, the attendant could take them on to the autism classroom for the remainder of the time.

If you have a children's church program during Sunday morning services, this may also serve as an alternate activity. For example, children with autism may be able to attend children's church for fifteen minutes or so while they are doing music before returning to their special classroom. This will also allow the children to be around typical children for a peri

Adequate Staff or Attendants for the Children
It is absolutely necessary that the family of a child with autism kno your autism classroom is adequately staffed. Your church will ne

of rotating helpers to staff the room and care for the child's needs during services. Inform the parents each week who is caring for their child. A few tips for staffing the room include:

- *Two or More Attendants.* It is a very good idea to have two people supervising the child with autism at all times. If problems should arise, one person can go get help or perhaps keep the situation under control. Some children with milder autism may be fine with one attendant, but you will be able to determine that only after interacting with the child for a while or obtaining specific advice from the child's parents.

- *Willing Workers.* People who serve in this area need to be willing. Do not coerce people to work in the autism classroom if they are very uncomfortable about doing something like this. Of course, some individuals will be a little hesitant but later discover how rewarding the service is. They might realize they have hidden talents for ministry to children with autism. If the attendants know how to occupy the child and feel adequately trained before they start, they will be more apt to step up and try. It's often fear of the unknown that prevents people from trying new things. Also, for several different reasons, I advise that you not enlist new church members for this work until they have been a part of your church body for a while.

- *Enlist the men of your church.* Men are often very good at working with children who have autism, and these children often respond well to them. Some men would never be very good at caring for tiny babies in the nursery but would shine with a child dealing with autism. Men also have more physical strength, making them a great match for dealing with older children.

- *Husband-and-wife teams.* Couples are often a great choice for working with a child with autism. The same balancing elements that take place in the home benefit their church ministry with these children. What one spouse doesn't understand, the other spouse often does.

- *Older teenagers.* The suitability of using teens for this ministry will be determined by the level or severity of a child's autism, but teens are often a good fit for this type of ministry. Older teenagers (i.e., seventeen years old or older) can watch a child with autism if they are well trained. One way of learning which teens are best suited for this service is to have them partner with an older, seasoned person for a probation-ary period. They can ask all the questions they want while they observe how the child behaves and how to respond to the child. Remember, God often calls people to work with the handicapped while they are still in their teenage years. If any teenager is interested in helping with this ministry, find a way to get her or him involved.

- *College-age people.* Many times college-age people are unmarried or don't have children of their own yet, but they have plenty of energy to help with a child with autism. Most churches have members who are college students. In addition, college students who are studying for special-education degrees will likely jump at the chance to help in the autism classroom. This is a great opportunity for them to experience what it is like to work hands-on with a child with autism. They may even use the time as service credit for their college classes. If your church solicits help from a local college for this ministry, you should take time to do a background check on each student. This protects the child from harm and your church from liability.

- *Special-Education Professionals.* Many churches have church members who work professionally in the special education field. Though it might seem natural to choose them to help in this area, I would issue a word of caution in this regard. While they can be of tremendous help in designing the room's environment and setting it up, I would not rely on them too much to work in the room on a continual basis. Special education is a very demanding occupation. If they are already doing this on a daily basis during the week, they need a break on the week-ends. However, their expertise can be of great value while training others in the church and in properly equipping the room.

Educate and Inform the Attendants

Never put someone to work with a child with autism until you have taken the time to sit down with the person to discuss the child's needs and any details specific to that child. Remember, this child is likely different from any child he or she has watched before. If the child is nonverbal and uses alternate means to show what he or she wants, this information must be shared. Attendants need to feel some level of confidence in what they are doing in order to get the best possible results from the program.

The parents of children with autism must be involved in training the attendants. Nobody knows the child like the parents. Personally, I like things written down and feel a parent's homemade notebook about the child would be the best approach. The notebook should cover everything from how to give the child verbal commands, to how to react when the child is upset, to how to deal with dietary issues, as well as any other specific things that only parents would know. Pages can be added as time passes and new issues arise. Photos of the child, the church building, their family, and so on would add meaning to the book. Copies of the notebook could be given to everyone who works with the child. The workers could take it home, read it, and ask any questions prior to working with the child. Make sure the parents' contact information is included in the book, should a worker want to discuss anything with them. Good communication between workers and the family is an absolute must. A copy of the notebook should remain in the autism classroom at all times in case a worker needs to reference it.

A Pager Device

This device is optional, but it can give new workers peace of mind in working with the child, despite any reservations they might have. You may actually be able to enlist some new workers just because of this little device. The pager device could be handed to the parents to carry during services. If a worker becomes overwhelmed and really thinks they have no other recourse, they could page the parents to come for the child. Most parents would rather have someone admit they need to be relieved than discover that things spiraled out of control. It's better to prevent a bad situation from escalating into a worse situation, because this will set the tone for the family's future visits to church. Parents of children with autism will readily excuse themselves early from church service and head home with the child if necessary. We know that autism is an unpredictable roller-coaster and sometimes we just have to call it a day. Interruptions are a normal part of our lives, and we are not offended when they occur.

Give the Autism Classroom a Name

Lastly, I recommend giving the classroom a special name, something positive or scriptural to give hope to the families of these children. Names such as "Haven of Hope," "God's Oasis," or "The Rainbow Room" lend a touch of God's grace while leaving the word autism out. Most of us parents see that word often enough, and it will be refreshing to hear words of hope instead. Leaving the word *autism* out of the room's name also suggests that children with other handicaps or disabilities are also welcome. Besides, if word gets out that your church is ready to meet the needs of children with autism, it won't matter what the room is called. You will be known as a church ready to minister.

It may take your church a while to establish a system such as this one. Problems may need to be resolved and details ironed out. Eventually, your church will get the hang of it, and the autism ministry will assume a life of its own. However long it takes your church to accomplish this, the ministry will be well worth it to families whose lives are broken by autism.

If you currently have no families of children with autism in your church, it would still be good to consider what you would do if such a family showed up for services or desired to come to your church. Have a tentative plan in place for serving such a family on that first day. In addition, it is a good idea to have a plan for an autism classroom on the drawing board in case a member of your church invites a family of a child with autism to start attending your services. Just knowing the prevalence of autism is good reason to ponder what your church will do in response.

Perhaps your city or community already has a number of children with autism. If so, it would be a good idea to go ahead and get the autism classroom started and advertise it to the public. You might be surprised at the response. Many families of children with autism aren't in church but really want to be. One young mother recently told me she has craved God so much more since her son's diagnosis of autism but found it so discouraging to sit in church alone while her husband stayed home each Sunday with their son.

As word of this ministry spreads, your congregation may be able to meet the needs of more than one family with autism. You may need to increase the number of workers in the autism classroom. If so, consider it your church's calling from God and go with it. There are so many places that families of children with autism cannot go, but church should not be one of them. The movie *Field of Dreams* made famous the catch phrase, "If you build it, they will come." The same will hold true for your church's response to autism: If you build such a ministry, they will come.

If you are part of a small congregation, you may wonder how an autism program could fit into the picture. I admit that some of what I've outlined would need to be scaled back in a church body of less than one hundred people. But this doesn't mean your church can't do something to minister to a child with autism. I would suggest that you start small and do what you can. For instance, offer care to the child with autism for worship services only; if that program succeeds over time, you could offer care during the Sunday school hour as well. Most parents understand that your church can't do it all, and they will be thrilled with any thoughtful help you can offer. Some of the easier tips, such as offering help at church dinners and household help, might make your ministry to the family more complete. A scaled-back version of care is much better than nothing at all. If this is how you need to start, I recommend that you not advertise your program to the public but concentrate on serving the child or children with autism whose families already have interest in coming to your church

I was glad when they said to me,
"Let us go into the house of the Lord."
—Psalm 122:1

What About Inclusion?

Most children with autism are in schools where they strive for inclusion in typical settings or areas where normal children are learning. In addition to attending special classes, the children are taken to other settings to mingle with their typical peers. The is done because the child with autism learns to emulate normal behaviors by being in those settings. If this is the case with the child your church is ministering to and the parents desire to see some inclusion, then by all means give it a try. It could be something as simple as making sure the child has an attendant to accompany him or her to Sunday school and to guide the child to the autism classroom during church services. If this turns out not to be workable on some days, the child can always go to the autism classroom as Plan B.

The Sunday school teachers in each case need to be aware that the child will be a part of their class and should be trained in caring for children with autism. Some teachers will have a knack with these kids, while others will need to be told specifically how to respond. If the Sunday school teachers have a copy of the child's notebook (discussed earlier in this chapter), this will greatly help in educating them. What's most important is this: attendants who stay with children with autism must know their needs and abilities. (By the way, you may choose to call the attendant by other titles if you like, such as "shadow" or "helper.")

Including the child in any special events will be important to some parents. If the parents long to see their child doing something with normal or typical children, try your hardest to help make it happen. For example, if your church is presenting a children's Christmas program, perhaps a short part could be given to the child with autism. Besides meeting one of the parents' important objectives, this would give the child a sense of accomplishment. If the child is verbal, he or she could speak a sentence or just a few words in the script. If the child is nonverbal, assign a nonspeaking part, even if it puts the child on stage for only a minute. A musical program may be another way to include a child with autism if the child can stand with the group for any length of time. Even if the child can't sing, it will bless the family to see their child included. Some autistic children love to stand at the door and hand out programs. Just seeing their child dressed up or in a costume will create a moment the family can photograph and treasure.

Naturally, all of these ideas hinge on the child's level of autism and abilities. Some children will clearly be unable to do anything like these. But if it is possible, involving a child with autism in the activities of other children would encourage the family and is well worth the effort. Even if you try and fail, the parents will be touched to realize that someone cared enough to try. Any inclusion in a special event will require an attendant to supervise the child.

Vacation Bible school is another possibility for including the child with autism, but it will require planning to make it happen. VBS is known for fast-moving activities, music, and doing things on a tight schedule. On the other hand, the autistic child's noises and disruptions might be less of a distraction here. The principle of having an attendant for the child at all times also applies to VBS. In addition, a parent needs to be available for early pick-up should the child become tired and unable to cope.

Offering Extra Help at Church Events

After you've come to minister to a child with autism and discover how much is involved with his or her care, you will also find that it's a physically demanding responsibility. Most children with autism cannot be left alone for any length of time due to the safety issues. (They have no natural fear.) You truly have to keep an eye on them at all times. With this in mind, it is always good to have help for social events at church, such as a picnic, church social, or banquet. Many parents of children with autism literally eat in shifts when they attend a special occasion. One parent sits and eats quickly while the other parent watches the child. Offering to monitor the child with autism during the meal portion of a church event is a great service to the family.

> *Then He also said to him who invited Him, "When you give a dinner or a supper, do not ask your friends, your brothers, your relatives, nor rich neighbors, lest they also invite you back, and you be repaid. But when you give a feast, invite the poor, the maimed, the lame, the blind. And you will be blessed, because they cannot repay you; for you shall be repaid at the resurrection of the just."*
> —*Luke 14:12–14*

Educating the Congregation

This chapter is primarily for those who will work directly with the child with autism, but some people in your congregation cannot be directly involved in the ministry to these families, for a variety of reasons. However, you should educate those people as well about the implications of autism. I believe there is a great need for everyone in your congregation to welcome the child with autism. That requires some education and the removal of fear. Unreasonable fear can lead to panic, and panic can cause a poor outcome for the child with autism in your church body.

Autism is often discussed on the evening news, but it is still mysterious to the average citizen. The fact that each child with autism is unique adds to the mystery. People cannot simply read a magazine article about one child's autism and have a fair picture of what all autism looks like. One child with autism may be able to talk and communicate, while another cannot communicate or may be more physically disabled by the disorder. For these reasons, the needs of each child with autism should be explained to the church so that worshipers feel they understand the child and know what to expect when the child is present.

I recommend that you address this in a personalized letter introducing the child to the entire church. The letter could be included with the church's newsletter to make sure everyone who might encounter the child at church gets the information. Enlist the parents' help in writing this letter of introduction, because it should include only the information they want it to contain. Any of the child's obvious autism symptoms—including communication abnormalities, behaviors, obsessions, likes or dislikes—should be described in the letter. I also recommend that a photo of the child be printed in the letter so that church members will recognize the child when they meet. See the sample introduction letter included on the following pages; feel free to alter it or add other ideas of your own:

Sample Letter

Dear Church Family,

We at Community Fellowship Church would like to take a few moments to let you know of someone extra special who is now attending our church. Her name is Elizabeth Morris.* Elizabeth and her family just moved here from the state of Florida and look forward to being part of our community and our church. Elizabeth is 12 and is part of a loving family. Her parents are George and Sandy Morris, and she has two siblings, Jonathan (age 10) and David (age 16).

What makes Elizabeth extra-special is the fact that she has autism, and this is the reason for this letter. Autism is becoming more and more common, yet each person with autism is very different.

We decided to let you know more about Elizabeth by way of this letter so that you will feel like you know her before you meet her. Please read the attached letter and have a wonderful day.

In Christ Jesus,

Pastor signature

Elizabeth Marie Morris (also called "Lizzy" by her family)
    Age 12
    Birthday: October 1
    Diagnosed with autism at age 3.
    Elizabeth is 4' 10" and has sandy brown hair. She looks very much like
    her mother and is proud of that fact.

Level of Autism

Elizabeth has been diagnosed with a moderate level of autism, which affects her in a variety of ways. The greatest impact on her life is the struggle to communicate. Elizabeth also suffers with sensory issues that affect her sense of wellness on a daily basis. Despite the autism, Elizabeth has a bright personality and is very lovable in so many ways. She has a dog named Lucky and will enjoy showing you his picture if you ask her. Elizabeth is enrolled in our public school system and spends much of her day in the special education wing of the school. Her teacher is Mrs. Smith, who has taught special-needs students for many years.

Communication Abilities

Elizabeth is nonverbal and uses a variety of methods to communicate. She can use sign language to indicate yes and no. She is able to point to things and expresses likes and dislikes very well with facial expressions. Sometimes Elizabeth writes down what she wants if she is having a good day. Although Elizabeth does not speak, she still understands most of what is spoken to her. Please feel free to say hello to her when you see her at church. She may or may not look at you, but she definitely hears you and likes being greeted. Elizabeth does fairly well with the alternative methods of communication that she uses, but sometimes she cannot convey what she wants. On these occasions, she may get frustrated and upset.

Sensory Issues

Elizabeth can be very sensitive to touch, and her sensitivity varies a great deal from day to day. Sometimes she may desire to be touched, but often she does not like it. If she gets close enough to touch you, this means she doesn't mind being touched casually on that day. Regarding hugs, which we all are accustomed to giving at our church: Do not hug Elizabeth until you ask her permission first. If you ask and she steps forward toward you, this is your cue that it is okay to hug her. If she ignores you or backs away, don't try to hug her that day. (It's not that she dislikes hugs or affection, but rather that her sensory needs are very different from day to day.)

Also, due to Elizabeth's sensory disturbances, she may begin "stimming," which many people with autism do to stimulate their brains. Stimming is a combination of body motions: Elizabeth will rock forward somewhat and flap her hands while making an unusual noise with her mouth. Do not let this alarm you; this is completely normal for her. She often will do this if she is excited, sometimes if she is upset, and occasionally for no apparent reason at all.

Dietary Issues

Elizabeth is on a no-dairy diet, which her family manages quite well. Be cautious about offering candy to her, as some of it may have dairy ingredients. If you want to offer candy to Elizabeth, ask her parents first, as they usually know which candies are dairy-free. (For all those who keep candy in their purses or pockets: Elizabeth loves Starlight Peppermint candies and can eat them without any problem.)

Elizabeth's Personal Favorites

Elizabeth loves baseball and already has a few strong team preferences. She loves the Chicago Cubs and will probably wear some Cubs sportswear to church. She loves to hear others talk about her favorite team. So, if you are a Cubs fan, you already have plenty to talk to Elizabeth about. But if they lose, she might be grouchy!

Obsessions You May See

Elizabeth has a few obsessions you should be aware of. She has a fixation on zippers and believes that zippers should always be zipped shut. If she notices a zipper on a lady's purse that isn't zipped, she may walk over and zip it up. Sometimes people wear jackets into church which are halfway zipped. In this case, Elizabeth may approach you and try zipping your jacket all the way up. Please do not be offended; this is simply an obsession she can't control. Either zip it for her or allow her to zip it up. When she walks out of sight, feel free to adjust the zipper to your liking and she will probably not notice.

Elizabeth is also very fond of the Nike swoosh logo. If she notices that your clothing has the Nike logo, she will probably spot you in a crowd and follow you closely. If she gets too close to you, simply ask her to move back and tell her she's too close. She will understand.

Things That May Upset Elizabeth

Elizabeth is greatly affected by thunderstorms. Her family is unsure if she is disturbed by the noise of the thunder, the lightning, the change in atmospheric pressure connected to the storm, or some other factor. Regardless of the cause, thunderstorms are unbearable for Elizabeth. Her autism will be much worse on stormy days. Take a moment to pray for Elizabeth on any day we have thunderstorms and be especially compassionate toward her and her family if one should arise while we are at church.

Change is also something Elizabeth finds very hard to cope with. Changes we make at church may affect her. Anything we alter, such as putting up Christmas decorations or rearranging chairs for a baptism, could affect her mood. Her family is always trying to help Elizabeth find better ways to cope with changes that the rest of us take for granted, but this remains an area of difficulty. Sometimes warning Elizabeth that something will be different is enough to help her cope with change. We can all help by letting Elizabeth's family know of changes we plan to make at church.

Behavior Issues That May Arise

Any of Elizabeth's autism symptoms could produce a behavior problem, although most are containable and her parents do a good job of keeping things under control. However, if you see some behavior that concerns you, her family would like to know. Since Suzy Smith is a close friend of the family, we've arranged for her to be the contact person for any problems you might encounter with Elizabeth at church. If something concerns you, call Suzy and she will bring the issue to the Morris family on your behalf.

We hope this little sketch of Elizabeth is helpful to you and your family. Take time to read it with your family. In particular, be sure to let your children know about Elizabeth and her special needs so that they will feel informed as well. All of us at Community Fellowship Church need to learn to love each other, even those afflicted with unfamiliar disabilities. Let's all look for Elizabeth and her family next time we meet and make them all feel welcome.

—Welcoming Committee Staff of
Community Fellowship Church

* *Elizabeth Morris, her story, and all names and circumstances are fictional and given for example purposes only.*

A Specific Example

All of the ideas for ministry in this chapter require organization, sincere love, dedication, and a heart for service. I hope God is glorified and people's needs are met as your church stretches itself in faith to do what the Lord calls you to do. The rewards will be endless and will be counted in the next world to come.

It may seem like a daunting task to create such a program, but other churches have done this and found it very rewarding. A good example is Deltona Lakes Baptist Church in Deltona, Florida. This church has created a ministry called Two By Two especially for children with autism. Two By Two is based on the Bible's story of Noah, who took all creatures into the ark two by two. It emphasizes the biblical truth that we are all better together and no one should be left behind. The Two By Two ministry is a natural expression of a core value that the congregation embraces as a whole body: "Love God and Love People." They have found their church motto in Matthew 22:37–40:

> *Jesus said to him, "'You shall love the L*ORD* your God with all your heart, with all your soul, and with all your mind.' This is the first and great commandment. And the second is like it: 'You shall love your neighbor as yourself.' On these two commandments hang all the Law and the Prophets."*

Deltona Lakes Baptist Church took this a step farther than most congregations when they decided to create their Two By Two ministry to include children with autism in their church life. The program strives to mainstream these children into regular, age-appropriate classrooms while also maintaining a separate classroom with special educational activities for the times when mainstreaming isn't possible. They assign each child with autism a "Bible Buddy," an attendant who accompanies the child everywhere in the church building. The idea for the Two by Two ministry came from a couple that still attends Deltona Lakes Baptist Church, Tim and Sheila Downs. Sheila says, "Tim and I felt God was leading us to do this ministry. We went to our pastor and he was completely on board. We then went in front of the church, shared our story, and told them about the huge need to open our hearts to these families."

The Two by Two program began with two children with autism and has had as many as eight children involved at one time or another.

Currently, the ministry serves the needs of three children with autism ranging in age from six years old to fifth grade. However, the congregation is also prepared to serve the needs of high-school-age youth with autism. I asked Sheila Downs how the Two by Two ministry has affected their church. She said, "I think that it has been a huge help to our children and their families in the ministry. Friendships between families have also grown. I also think that it opened people's eyes to the increasing numbers of children who have autism. Although our program only services a few autistic children at the present time, we found the program to be highly valuable to our church." I also asked Sheila if she felt the Two by Two program had given the Deltona Lakes Baptist church body any unique blessings. She replied, "Absolutely! We have seen our typical kids in classes take it upon themselves to befriend our Two by Two kids. They know that when we love God, we need to love ALL people. We know this is what Jesus expects of us."

Later, I questioned Sheila about the personal fulfillment and blessing she and her husband Tim have received through this ministry. She replied, "Seeing these children able to come to church and experience the love of Christ is awesome. Our parents have been incredible, and we all work well together. We love to hear how the children are excited to come to church. We had one parent share a story about a particular Sunday morning when she was sick and not planning on coming to church. Her son had made up his mind that he was not going to stay home. He told his Mom to 'call Mr. Tim and tell him to pick me up.' We really weren't sure that we were making very much progress with that particular child, so that was a huge blessing to hear! Every one of our volunteers has shared how much it has meant to them to work with their particular child. We have watched people completely step out of their comfort zones and truly be blessed by God."

This chapter ends with thanks to God for the inspiration and directive we find in 1 Corinthians 12:22–26. Deltona Lakes Baptist Church's ministry to children with autism is a modern-day expression of an important truth regarding the church body that we find in this passage of God's Word.

On the contrary, those parts of the body that seem to be weaker are indispensable, and the parts that we think are less honorable we treat with special honor. And the parts that are unpresentable are treated with special modesty, while our presentable parts need no special treatment. But God has combined the members of the body and has given greater honor to the parts that lacked it, so that there should be no division in the body, but that its parts should have equal concern for each other. If one part suffers, every part suffers with it; if one part is honored, every part rejoices with it.

—*1 Corinthians 12:22–26* NIV

CHAPTER 9

Ministering to Families with Special Circumstances

W hile the story you've read about our life and journey with autism may sound more unusual and trying than anything you've ever encountered, let me tell you there are even more trying situations than ours. Sometimes the child with autism will be part of what I call "special circumstances" in which the need to minister will either be greater or need to be fine-tuned to fit the situation. With that in mind, please read further in the event that the child to whom you want to minister is part of such special circumstances.

Single-Parent Households

After reading how difficult autism can be to overcome and adapt to in a family, you understand the toll it can take on a marriage. It's a serious strain. Some divorces happen early on due to one parent's inability to cope with the diagnosis of autism and the lifelong prognosis. It's not unheard of for one parent to divorce the other within the first few years of the onset of autism. In some cases, the wife or the husband will say that they grew apart over the years due to the physical demands of the autism and the lack of time for the marital relationship. Some reports place the divorce statistic as high as 80 percent for marriages dealing with a child with autism. I've often wondered, had those same families been physically helped and ministered to, might they have stayed together? I'm grateful to be able to say that of the parents of children with autism whom I know, the majority have stayed together. However, I am not ignorant of the statistic that points in the other direction.

Some single-parent families of children with autism are mothers who have never been married. Their stories are often one of autism compounded by poverty; they frequently struggle with the inability to seek out the care they really want for their children with autism. These single parents may hear of the newer treatments or natural treatments available for autism but be unable to financially bear that expense.

Can you imagine bearing this load without a spouse? For example, in the father's chapter of this book, I shared how fathers of children with autism fall seriously behind on their work around the home and yard. Can you imagine not having a husband yet having a house to keep up, as well as trying to meet the special needs of a child with autism? Can you imagine being the single father of a child with autism while having to deal with issues that women are normally better at? Can you imagine having no spouse to discuss decisions with after coming home from a school meeting regarding your child's care? All the issues of autism and the struggles involved are simply compounded for single parents. If you seek to minister to one of these precious families, I believe God is truly calling you.

All of the ministry ideas in this book could be used with a family lacking one parent or the other, but they might need to be stepped up a level due to the potentially desperate nature of the situation.

To effectively minister to a single-parent household, you must become involved with the family on a personal level to discover their greatest needs. For example, you might find that a single mother of a child with autism already has neighbors or family who tend to her lawn, but she may be desperate for help with keeping the housework up or even having a sitter who can watch the children so she can go out by herself. After you get to know the family's greatest needs, you will probably need to network with other Christians to get things done. Many of the chapters in this book deal with networking and asking others to help in specific ways, and the case of a single parent household clearly needs such an approach.

If the family you are ministering to happens to live in your neighborhood, do not be afraid to ask others nearby to network with you on whatever level they can. Often, people really want to help, but fear holds them back. Some people desire to help but just need someone to formally ask them. Some people are leaders and some people are followers, but they follow very well. Don't be afraid to ask and don't be afraid to be a leader if God is giving you eyes to see a burden and a heart that wants to help.

Help for the family might be a stone's throw from their own front door. For example, a family next-door with teenagers might help with washing windows, while an older retired couple helps put together a home-cooked meal or helps with the siblings in some way. If you have older children who are capable of helping in some way, this is the perfect opportunity to teach them to serve others in dire need.

You can enlist people from your own church body, but don't forget to think of people outside your church. Enlist the help of Christians who attend other churches as well as other groups who may also care. There are also civic organizations in nearly every community. They might be willing to help with a task on your list. For example, a single mother may need help with lawn mowing, and a men's organization may take turns getting it done.

If God has laid the family on your heart, it could be that you are the one to step into the home, get to know the family personally, and then enlist the proper help. Many times, all it takes is a request from somebody to meet a need. Pray for God's guidance through every step. If you ever get to the point where you don't feel you can handle it, ask others to join with you in organizing help.

> *When the ear heard, then it blessed me,*
> *And when the eye saw, then it approved me;*
> *Because I delivered the poor who cried out,*
> *The fatherless and the one who had no helper.*
> *The blessing of a perishing man came upon me,*
> *And I caused the widow's heart to sing for joy.*
> *—Job 29:11–13*

Families with More Than One Autistic Child

This situation takes my breath completely away when I hear of it. Although I do not personally know anyone who has more than one child with autism, I've seen a few families on television or read magazine articles describing families with two or more children with autism. If you know such a family, I can tell you that they really do need help. I compare this to the years we've survived in our house and how we needed so much help with just one child with autism. If I try to double or triple the burden in my imagination, I just can't wrap my mind around it.

As always, you must take time to get to know the family. Show them you care. Take time to get to know each child as an individual; be cautious, understanding that siblings with autism may be very different from each other and each have their own set of autistic symptoms. Learning the family dynamics is critical. For example, one family may live near many relatives and have a great deal of help available at a moment's notice while another family may have no relatives or friends to help. A family with more than one child with autism will likely need some help even if they have a good support system. Your offer to help the family will be a testimony not only to them but to their families who are doing all they can. Do whatever you can, even if it starts with a hot meal brought to their door or an offer to wash windows in the spring.

Love does no harm to a neighbor; therefore love is the fulfillment of the law.
—Romans 13:10

Families Who Don't Know Jesus as Savior

As a parent, I am most grateful for my salvation, which came through the blood of Christ. My husband and I were already Christians when our son was born, and although it has been a difficult situation for everyone in my family, it has been our faith in Christ that has carried us this far. We truly couldn't have borne the weight of this burden without the Holy Spirit, who led us through the darkest hours of this journey. Only by looking at autism through the lens of faith could we carry the burden with grace. I shudder to think what souls without the Lord do to cope with autism in their family.

Perhaps the family you desire to minister to are not Christians and have no idea what genuine faith looks like. You have a virtual goldmine of spiritual opportunity right before your eyes. What if the family has doubted God's very existence due to the fact they are suffering terribly and nobody has even acquainted themselves with their sorrow? Your presence and support in their lives will be an undeniable grace walking through their front door. Your offer to help in whatever way you feel led will shine God's love through to their hearts, where they are the most desperate. It could be that God is using the autism to intersect your life with theirs and ultimately lead to their salvation in Christ. You might be the first Christian who has offered to help them in any way. We never know what God will use to reveal Himself to a lost world.

Nonbelievers may be a bit shy about accepting help since the servant mentality may be foreign to them. Be sensitive: they may welcome your help in some areas but may feel that you are intruding in others. For example, they may love help with yard work but would be offended by a financial gift. Everyone is different. You will learn to take cues from them as you offer help. Walk through the doors that are welcome and don't push through any doors where you are not. If your church creates an autism classroom (described in chapter 8), then you can invite the family to your church. They may or may not accept your offer. But don't stop your love and service to them if they don't accept your invitation. Take Jesus to them every time you enter their home.

Start slowly with spiritual encouragement, but be careful not to leave it out. For example, in chapter 6 of this book, you will find a section outlining how to pray God's Word and create prayers with the child's name inserted. This is a wonderful gesture to start with and will likely touch a family that is not Christian. If they are really responsive to that gesture, the gift of a Bible for the home could follow next, followed by a praise and worship CD. Build slowly. If they are being drawn by the Spirit, they will start asking you questions of a spiritual nature. If they ask you questions regarding God's reasoning for allowing autism, do not feel you have to conjure up answers. Rather, let them know that you don't know the answer, but remind them of what is solid and unchanging, and that is God's sovereignty and grace and His provision of salvation through Christ. The family may not understand God as you do, but they will not be able to deny His interest in their lives, simply because of your presence and help. You will become a tangible blessing, which could open up the doors of understanding for them.

Now thanks be to God who always leads us in triumph in Christ, and through us diffuses the fragrance of His knowledge in every place. For we are to God the fragrance of Christ among those who are being saved and among those who are perishing. To the one we are the aroma of death leading to death, and to the other the aroma of life leading to life. And who is sufficient for these things? For we are not, as so many, peddling the word of God; but as of sincerity, but as from God, we speak in the sight of God in Christ.
—2 Corinthians 2:14–17

CHAPTER 10

Lessons to Learn

Learning to Laugh at What's Funny

Someone might read a story such as ours and think there's nothing in our experience to laugh at. But they would be wrong. After living with autism for a while, family members learn to laugh about certain things. This might seem an odd thing to say as you read of all the heartache described in this account, but some things autistic people do can really crack you up. We consider it God's way of giving us a break from the tension. Sometimes I compare stories with another parent of an autistic child and find myself saying, "No, wait! You have to hear what my son does!" Laughter is one of the most healing things for the human spirit. I firmly believe that God has given us…

> *A time to weep,*
> *And a time to laugh;*
> *A time to mourn,*
> *And a time to dance.*
> *—Ecclesiastes 3:4*

Our son Taylor makes some of the funniest faces. (Some medical experts call this behavior the "autistic grimace.") He can wince his eyes halfway closed and look just like Festus from the old television show *Gunsmoke*. Sometimes we will be telling Taylor something very serious and he will raise his eyebrows to make an expression that dissolves any seriousness we were trying to accomplish. When he makes these faces, it's not at all uncommon for one of us to run laughing from a room, our hands over our mouths. Frankly, we wonder at times if he makes funny faces just to get out of trouble. We can't tell, so we just laugh and end up working on the issue at another time.

Sometimes Taylor does the oddest little things that are comical. He has developed the habit of picking one person in a crowd or family gathering. He then goes up to them, puts his eyes as close to their eyes as he can get (often touching forehead to forehead), and then giggles. Once a person figures out what he's up to, they laugh too. We say that they are the "chosen one" for the day, because Taylor will go back repeatedly to the same person and do it all over again.

Most people with autism have little or no sense of modesty and need to be taught and reminded to cover up or put clothes back on. This is a constant problem in our house. I recall the big birthday party we had in Taylor's honor one year, the house full of relatives eating and making conversation throughout the front room and kitchen area. Taylor decided to use the toilet in the laundry room just off the kitchen. As he often does, he got his underwear a little wet in the process, so he took his clothes off and walked totally naked right through the house in front of his birthday guests. My brother Terry yelled, "Don't look, Ethel! It's a streaker!" I panicked and scrambled around for something to cover him. But we all got a good laugh. When we recall that incident, we joke that Taylor needed to show us his birthday suit on his birthday.

Taylor has also gone outside with few clothes on. One hot summer he was in the habit of wearing only his underwear in the house, although he learned to put on shorts if he ventured outside. Well, one day this slipped his mind. I looked out one window while doing my housework. There was Taylor, big as life, strolling around our property in his underwear. I ran like a bullet to get him back inside. The entire time I was running after him, my eyes were scanning the street and neighbors' yards to see who might have caught a glimpse of what was happening. When I finally got him back inside, I fell flat on the couch and burst out laughing uncontrollably.

Speaking of neighbors, I must have some of the nicest ones on the planet. Most neighbors would consider breaking and entering an offense worthy of causing a neighborhood feud. But several of mine continue to chuckle over Taylor's invasion of their homes one summer. This was one of those time periods that began with a very distinct obsession and grew into something where the "ornery normal kid" side of Taylor came out.

Sometime in the spring of that year, Taylor became very obsessed with clocks, not just any clocks, but the more old-fashioned kind with a clock face, especially the ones with a swinging pendulum. We began noticing that there were occasions when Taylor would perk up immediately as we drove past particular houses. Driving more slowly and looking more closely, we realized that these houses had a clock on the wall that Taylor noticed, capturing his attention, even passing by in the car.

The house on the corner of our subdivision (diagonal from ours out our backyard) had a clock on the living room wall. I saw several times as we passed it that Taylor was intrigued. Taylor soon expressed interest in getting much closer to that house, inching his way to the corner of our backyard that angled closest to their backyard, staring longingly at their home.

One particular afternoon, both Taylor and I were out in the backyard together. Taylor started walking quickly toward the backyard of that house but turned around and made full eye contact with me first. Once he got it, he tossed his head back in laughter and darted like a bullet for the house. I was hot on his heels in pursuit, but not fast enough to prevent what happened next.

Taylor entered that house and went right over and sat on the couch as if he had belonged there his whole life. I opened the sliding door and began chiding him to get out of there because it wasn't his house. He continued to giggle and went rigid on me, as if to say, "Not unless you make me, Momma." Smiling, the neighbor told me over and over that it was okay as I pushed and pulled him off the couch. I was utterly embarrassed, but she kept reassuring me that she wasn't upset. At one point, I got him on his back and began pulling him toward the sliding door by his ankles. He giggled the entire way across the carpet. Just as we were about to get out of her door, he grabbed onto the frame of the sliding doors, preventing me from final victory. I asked my neighbor to pry his fingers off the door frame so I could get him out. She was able to prod his knuckles, causing him to release his grip, and I was finally able to get him out of her house.

As we trotted back to our house across the backyards, I raked Taylor over the coals, letting him know that he had done something very bad and that he'd better never do it again. We were only about half way home, approaching our backyard, when Taylor made an abrupt left turn and darted toward another house! I was still panting from his first escapade, and now a second one was unfolding.

Taylor ran in that house, right past the woman who lived there, and down the basement steps as if he lived there and knew exactly where they were. I still don't know if he knew they had a family room at the bottom of those steps, but he went right to the couch and sat down like he'd done in the first house.

I tried my best to get him out of their basement, but I was worn out and no match for the energetic boy. The woman's husband came down the steps to help me. Taylor knew he was finally outnumbered. As together we tugged, Taylor continued to resist each step. Suddenly, I realized we needed to honor his obsession with light switches. I told the husband that if we both let go of Taylor and asked him to turn out the lights that he would do it and then come out willingly. That's exactly what happened. The neighbor was stunned that after all the tugging and pulling, a simple request to turn off the light was all it took to get Taylor to leave.

Not too many months later, I was having one of those days. I couldn't find Taylor anywhere. Going out to our yard, I walked the perimeter hunting for Taylor. Seeing the neighbor who had helped me extract Taylor from his basement, I asked if there was any possibility that Taylor was in their house. He chuckled and said, "Oh no! We lock our doors now!"

A merry heart makes a cheerful countenance,
But by sorrow of the heart the spirit is broken.
—Proverbs 15:13

People with autism have the attitude of "Who cares who sees this?" If they hear a song they like, they may just start dancing—in Wal-Mart, at a restaurant, or down the aisle of a grocery store. They have no fear of what people think. Sometimes I wonder if the rest of us would have a little more joy in our lives if we broke out dancing every now and then and forgot what people might think of it. We love the memory of Taylor attending a revival service one night at our church. Apparently, he liked the special music that evening. When the beat came through the speakers, we knew we were going to see something bizarre. No sooner had the thought entered our minds than Taylor stood up and began swaying back and forth in the pew, doing his little dance and bobbing his head. I looked around the congregation and saw hearts melting. There were smiles on people's faces. Sometimes revival starts in the least likely places.

Ever since Taylor was a toddler, he has been obsessed with the Missouri lottery. At first, he got very excited at the commercials on television when the numbered lottery balls came up the chute. As he got older, he knew the exact time Missouri's lottery drawing came on every night. He began doing something we came to call the lottery dance. The moment the commercial came on, he would trot around the living room in an exaggerated prance, waving his hands in the air. We watched it for years, thinking it was very funny.

One day, my sister Shelly was over visiting. She had never seen or heard of the lottery dance. I noticed on the wall clock that the lottery drawing was about to begin and told her she was about to be entertained. She had no clue what I meant, but I cleared the living-room floor in preparation.

The moment the commercial came on, Taylor took his cue and began circling the room, performing his little lottery dance. Shelly laughed till tears rolled down her face. Her reaction to seeing it for the first time was priceless. It was almost sad when Taylor stopped doing his lottery dance; we still consider it one of our fondest memories, and it's unlikely that my sister will ever forget it. Taylor now goes online to the lottery Web site and watches the daily drawing over and over to his heart's content. (We say that Taylor is probably the most lottery-obsessed person who has never purchased a ticket.)

Taylor can develop strange aversions to things for no apparent reason. In recent years, he decided he couldn't stand to hear anyone say the word *cheese*, nor could he bear to see pictures of cheese or even packages of cheese on the kitchen counter. (Oddly, he still likes to eat cheese on some foods.)

One day he was being a typical little brother and just giving Tyler a hard time. Taylor would dart into a room and poke Tyler on the shoulder, move the mouse while he was on the computer, and torment him in whatever way he could, all the while laughing at his own antics. Tyler had had his fill of this as Taylor was chasing him into the kitchen. Tyler suddenly got a bright idea. He pulled open the refrigerator, grabbed a box of Velveeta, and pointed it at Taylor. What happened next was unforgettable. Taylor saw the box of Velveeta and his entire countenance fell. He instantly stopped laughing, hung his head in defeat, and walked slowly out of the room. The brotherly battle was won with a box of cheese. Only at my house!

I have shared the sad and difficult story of what obsessive compulsive disorder did to our family, although at times Taylor's obsessions demonstrated a rigidity that was almost funny. So, we eventually learned to laugh a little at them. Taylor once decided that all persons who sat on the living room couch (including himself) could sit on only one couch cushion; no part of your body could cross the line where one cushion ended and the other began. I decided to test how carefully Taylor would observe this little rule in his head. One day he sat perfectly centered on his cushion while I sat on the cushion right next to him. After a few moments, I put one finger across the crack and waited to see if that was enough to trigger a reaction. It didn't take long. No sooner had we looked back and forth at each other when Taylor yelled at me. We all broke out in laughter and learned a valuable lesson: follow the rules, right down to the pinky finger!

Our son is considered nonverbal, although he tries very hard to get some words out. But children with autism who can speak may say the funniest things. My friend Donna's son is named Luke. One day they were in a church service when the priest asked the congregation to turn to the gospel of Luke in their Bibles. When Luke heard his name, he shot back, "Who? Me?" Donna says Luke continues to perk up every time their priest makes reference to the gospel of Luke, but she tells him, "It's another Luke, not you."

This chapter may have caught you off guard. Laughter? In a house with autism? Yes! We are still normal families underneath all the chaos of the problems that autism brings. And I felt the need to let you know that it's okay to laugh occasionally at things children with autism do. Granted, we don't laugh all the time, but when things are clearly hilarious, we do. We are not laughing at the fact our children have autism but rather at the gift of the humor that the unusual habits of kids with autism bring to the home. Trust me, we have enough heartache that an occasional funny moment is a great blessing. If the child with autism whom you are helping with does something really funny, it will not be a bad thing if you laugh along the way.

Go ahead and laugh. Chances are the child's parents have laughed at the same thing.

Learning What Not to Say

On the other hand, I would caution you that certain things should not be said to parents or family members of children with autism. Allow me to share some things I have collected over the years from conversations with other parents dealing with autism and from our own life.

When listening to the parent of a child with autism describe the troublesome behaviors or issues with which they are currently dealing, do not make an instant comparison to your own children and imply that you are dealing with the same thing. Many children with autism have behaviors that sound similar to behaviors of normal kids, but their behaviors rise to an abnormal level, becoming a significant hindrance or a hurdle to overcome. Mothers of children with autism have told me that they cringe when another mom waves her hand dismissively and says, "Oh, my kids do that too. It's no big deal!" Trust me when I say that the behavior of a child with autism is not the same. Avoid the temptation to feel obliged always to make a remark in response. Just be a good listener when parents of children with autism share their troubles.

Someone listening to a stressful story of autism will be tempted to ask, "What in the world are you going to do when your child gets bigger?" While this question certainly comes to mind, the parents will not have an answer, and just hearing it will not help. None of us even has the grace to face tomorrow. It comes from God's hand in daily doses, and believe me when I say that parents of children with autism live for daily grace.

Therefore do not worry about tomorrow, for tomorrow will worry about its own things. Sufficient for the day is its own trouble.
—Matthew 6:34

During particularly difficult times, parents of children with moderate to severe autism are often asked, "Have you ever thought about putting your child in a home or institution?" I call this the killer question. It kills a parent's spirit to hear that question and have to come up with an answer.

To give you an idea of the pain that question causes, you need to know that the parents welcomed their child into the family the same way you welcomed yours. They brought the child home from the hospital and expected that a normal life would unfold. They bonded with that child during the first year of life in the same way you have with yours. And while some parents eventually do make the difficult decision to place their child with autism in a home or facility, it is the most gut-wrenching decision of their lives. That decision will likely cause a season of grief much like they walked through at the time of diagnosis. So, I discourage you from asking that particular question unless you are prepared for the hurt it will cause. When you get the urge to ask it, stop and pray for the family instead.

To convey the gravity of this question, I sometimes ask the family of normal children to find their most recent family photo and ask themselves which of their kids they could put in a facility. It's a terrible thing to think of. People who ask this question usually seem to feel a desire to solve other people's problems. Upon hearing the details of a life with autism, they ask this question because they don't know how else to respond. They offer up what they believe might be a solution, supposing the parents may not have considered it.

Sometimes people make snap judgments that turn into a hurtful comment. While the public is coming to understand more about autism and the temper tantrums that come with it, some people are still oblivious to what is happening. Almost every parent of a child with autism has heard someone recommend stern discipline for the child's behavior.

It's not uncommon to hear someone say, "Are you sure they don't just need a good spanking?" or "I think I'd do something different with that child if I were you." The truth is, no normal person can understand what it's like to live in a body afflicted by autism. It takes most parents a long while (sometimes years) to learn what discipline will even work on a child with autism, so impulsive remarks from outsiders do not make the task any easier. Often the parents learn after a while exactly which behaviors are autism-related and which are controllable and need some correcting. Are we perfect? Do we always know what we're doing? Not a chance! But we are doing the best we can with the knowledge we have at the moment.

Sometimes a couple's first child is afflicted with autism, so they begin their new family with heartache. People are very curious and want to ask, "Do you think you will have any more kids?" Please don't ask that question. This is something the couple is already anguishing over in private; they don't need to ponder the answer with you. Many parents of children with autism will hesitate to have more children, and if subsequent children are born, they will be nervous throughout the pregnancy and the child's infancy until they truly believe the child is okay.

Many parents of children with autism feel isolated, misunderstood, and estranged from normal life. Sometimes they receive invitations from well-meaning friends or acquaintances but cannot accept them due to their responsibilities with the child living with autism. One mother told me she feels terrible when people don't understand that she cannot come to meetings and other events to which they invite her. They say, "Can't you get a sitter now and then?" or "Don't you ever get out?" These remarks cause a suffering family to suffer all the more. Most parents of children with autism have a totally different life than they once had and long for the normalcy they have lost. The truth is, most of us do not have a large pool of individuals able to handle our kids. We can't simply ask which teenagers in town are good babysitters like other families do. We do not get out often for this reason. If the grandparents have just watched our child so we could take our other children to a doctor's appointment or some other commitment, we can't turn around and ask them again when social occasions arise. When we turn down invitations or offers to go places, it's because we must sort out what we absolutely must do and what is optional. Please do invite us to these events, but please be understanding when we seldom come.

The most kind-hearted people will invite the parents to their home and say, "Just bring him with you; it's alright." While they are being truly hospitable and it isn't necessarily bad to invite the child with autism, we cannot bring our child to many settings. This can lead to misunderstandings, because the person inviting us doesn't truly understand why we decline. If our children with autism have obsessions, rituals, hyperactivity, or other behaviors that are likely to ruin an outing, then we have to decline. At other times, we are concerned that our children might break the hosts' valuable belongings. Some autistic children are so troubled by new settings that they will act out every time they are exposed to one. Sometimes they will be extra hyper in someone else's house, running from room to room on emotional overload. We wish we could just bring them with us anywhere we're invited, but there are valid reasons we cannot always do so.

Perhaps it can best be summarized in this way: We do love to be invited to social events and not feel left out, but we need an extra measure of compassion and understanding when we decline. Continue to invite us (and all of our children) because our child with autism may improve and we may be able to bring all our kids to your house one day. Just try to be understanding if we can't come now. For many families of children with autism, social gatherings are confined to the dinners they host in their own homes because it allows their child to be in his or her own familiar setting. Here's another idea: If you have repeatedly invited the family to your home for a meal and they decline to come, consider preparing a meal, loading it into your car, and taking it to them instead. This way the family gets the socialization they crave and you get to provide them with the lovely meal you had in mind. The parents may even have their child's sitter come over so they can enjoy your company.

Dear brothers, take note of this: Everyone should be quick to listen,
slow to speak and slow to become angry.
—James 1:19 NIV

AFTERWORD

I t's been great to have you join the Gosney family on our journey of autism and faith in Christ. I pray you have been blessed by the honesty and insight our story has offered as you read this book. It is also my hope that as you were enlightened on the subject of autism, that your heart will also be tender toward any family who has a child with any disability. This book was never intended to highlight autism as the only devastating disorder that can afflict a family. I've known many parents over the years with children who have disabilities other than autism, and I can tell you their burdens are great as well. Many of the ministry ideas contained in the chapters of this book could easily be used or adapted for other disabilities.

Although this book was written to teach Christians how to minister to autism, I realize that just about anyone might pick this book up, including some who do not yet know Christ as their personal Savior. You might be one of those individuals. Perhaps the spiritual tone of the book, the faith in Christ professed in the stories, or the scriptures scattered throughout, have left you searching your heart for something you believe is missing in your life. If this is how you feel, then I believe God is drawing you to himself and offering you what only he can offer. I encourage you to read the New Testament. My recommendation would be to read Matthew, Mark, Luke, John, Acts, and Romans. This will give you a clear picture of what Jesus did, His supreme sacrifice for you as an individual and for the world. If you read those chapters and find that you believe Jesus for everything that He is, bow before Him and cry out for your salvation. Just pour out everything you have to everything that He is. Ask Him to forgive your sin and come into your heart and life. It is a good idea to find a pastor in a Bible-believing church and ask for spiritual counseling to clarify any questions you still may have. You will also want to ask for believer's baptism and get grounded in a church where you can grow spiritually and know that God is honored and glorified above all else.

Farewell, my new friends!
God be with you all!
Sheila Gosney

APPENDIX A

The Symptoms and Treatment of Autism

Autism is classified as a severe developmental disorder affecting a large range of everyday movements, functions, and abilities. Autism can begin as early as birth or surface as late as a few years later. Some parents report children with autism to have been very docile and happy during infancy, while others claim nothing could make their child happy during the first year of life. Sometimes parents will tell you they had an idea something wasn't right with their child early on, while many others say their child seemed completely normal until a certain time and then autism suddenly began showing itself.

Children with autism can develop normally to a certain point and then suddenly regress, with the regression accompanied by a host of unusual behaviors that puzzle those who love them. Some autistic children have varying degrees of developmental delays during the first year of life, but often they are not seen as anything major, that is until later, when more problems are added to the developmental picture. Children with autism have been known to continually gain and lose skills, almost as if their brains forget the accomplishment even happened. This is perhaps one of the most heartbreaking aspects of autism for parents and educators alike.

For suggestions on resources that will help you better understand autism, see Appendix B.

What Is Autism?

The Umbrella of Autism: The Autism Spectrum

Doctors, therapists, and educators often speak of the autism spectrum or say that a child falls somewhere under the umbrella of autism. The reason for this is that autism has many different levels of severity and manifests itself in many different ways. Variations of autism include Kanner's autism, also known as classic autism; Asperger's syndrome; pervasive developmental disorder; as well as autism that is connected to other disorders. Some children have learning difficulties along with what is called a "brush of autism," which may impair them socially but still allow them to function at a fairly high level. Autism is a collection of symptoms that children will have, though not necessarily all at once. Some children may start out with one set of symptoms and develop others as time passes. But a certain number of autism symptoms tie the children with autism together. Medical doctors have a checklist of autism symptoms, and a child must register a certain number of symptoms to attain the diagnosis. I will attempt, in layman's terms, to describe some of the characteristics, symptoms, and treatments of autism so you can understand what goes on in the bodies of children with the disorder.

Sensory Problems

This aspect of autism may be the most common thread tying all children with autism together. Our sensory systems are all based on a fine network of neurotransmitters and nerves connected to the brain and responsible for a wide variety of body functions. Our sensory system includes tactile (touch), visual, oral (taste), auditory, and olfactory (smell). The sensory system is like a wiring network within the human body that is in constant use as we move through our day. For example, if you touch a surface that is too hot, a signal runs from your fingertips to the brain. The brain tells the fingers they are burning and sends a message down to the fingers, where you at once pull back after getting the signal.

All the senses, the entire sensory system, works this way, but we are totally unaware of how this process works if we are normal. Because the brain is affected by autism, the sensory system also suffers.

Some children with autism cannot stand to step on surfaces that have a strong sensory component, such as grass, cold marble floors, and different types of carpet. Other children with autism may crave sensations that another child with autism cannot stand. For example, one child can't bear to have his body touched by anyone, while another desires deep pressure applied to parts of his body.

Some children have visual disturbances with their autism, being very sensitive to sunlight, florescent lighting, or even fast moving video games. Some children lack normal pain responses, which can pose a health threat, especially if the child cannot sense when things are too hot and end up being seriously burned.

It is not uncommon to have children with autism so disturbed by sound that their mothers cannot run the vacuum sweeper unless the child is in another part of the house or out of the house entirely.

Other children with autism can handle noise in general but will be bothered by low noises others barely notice, such as the gentle sound of an air cleaner or a dishwasher. Sensory problems are common, they but differ greatly between the children. It's a matter of learning what bothers the child and working around it. Many of the therapy treatments children with autism receive are geared to help with sensory issues.

Stimulatory Behaviors

Certain behaviors are referred to as "stimming," meaning behaviors done to stimulate or make up for something missing in the brain. These are perhaps the most unusual-looking symptoms to the outside world when they first see a child with autism. Hand flapping and pacing are stimming behaviors. A child with autism may get excited (either happy or upset) and flap his or her wrists and hands repeatedly while making very throaty or guttural sounds. Some children will stim at the sight of their favorite logo, name brand, or television show. Other children will only stim when unhappy and agitated. Most parents of kids with autism will tell you from experience that stimming is very hard to control once it gets started. Some children stim quietly, flapping their hands and making a whisper-like sound, but many make very audible noises while stimming.

Many children with autism will stim by spinning either themselves around in circles or spinning objects. In their earliest days of autism, most children will turn toy cars upside-down so they can spin the wheels and watch the motion. This is often the first stimming sign of autism reported by parents. Some kids have the uncanny ability to spin objects nobody would dream could spin. They simply take an item, get it positioned in balance, give the wrist a whirl, and the item dances.

I once asked a doctor to explain stimming to me so I could understand it better. She said to think of an old-fashioned clock, one where you could see all the many cogs and wheels hitting one another to create the constant working motion. She told me the brain is much like the clock in the way that one thing hits the other to create a flow of motion. She explained that in the autistic brain, some "cogs" have nothing hitting them and the stimming behaviors make up for things that are missing. The child has no conscious thought or understanding of why they do the stimming; they just do it because it's a craving they can't control. The brain sends the impulse and the stimming begins.

Poor Eye Contact

People with autism generally have problems with eye contact. This can be an early symptom that something is wrong with a child. Some children can have eye contact that is good and then suddenly lose the ability to make eye contact as they revert into the painful world of autism. Some children will look at people only from a side view out of the corners of their eyes, while others will struggle with poor eye contact more on one day than another. Children with autism may squint more than typical children. They close their eyes until almost shut, all the while looking at the world through their eyelashes. Gaining good eye contact is a daily issue for those who educate children with autism.

Speech Delays, Speech Impediments, and Absence of Speech

Many children with autism have speech problems. Those with classic autism are more likely to have serious speech issues. Sometimes these can be overcome with a great deal of speech therapy; in other cases, the child can develop alternative ways to communicate, such as pointing to what they want, using special books with cards that help them communicate, or sign language. Some children use communication boards with success. Some children with autism eventually learn to write what they want on paper. Many children develop a mixture of different communicating methods, as if they are personalizing the way they communicate. The most devastating cases are when the child has not yet mastered any communication methods and remains frustrated every day, often causing tantrums from pent-up anger. One thing is for certain, children with autism often know exactly what it is they want; they just have to find ways to express it. This is perhaps one of the biggest misconceptions to the outside world. People see a child pacing, flapping his or her hands, making strange noises, and mistakenly believe the child is off in his or her own world with no connection to normal desires. But those who have children with autism will correct that notion very quickly. Another misconception is that because such children can't talk, they can't understand anything being said to them. Most kids with autism have a high receptive language understanding.

A knowledgeable doctor once said that to understand the awful feeling people with autism have when trying to communicate, you should think of the occasions where a word or thought is on the tip of your tongue but simply won't form, leaving you very frustrated in the moment. People with autism live with that same kind of frustration on a daily basis, if not moment to moment, especially if they struggle without any meaningful method of communication.

Children with Asperger's syndrome tend to have speech (though it often develops later), but they struggle to learn how to have appropriate conversations. Some speak very fast and have to be reminded to slow down. Others can speak well but have trouble speaking in social situations and difficulty carrying on a normal conversation with others. They have to be taught the normal social cues of conversation. Often, children with Asperger's can and will speak fluently on hot topics of personal interest. They will move through a crowd making conversation, finding ways to keep turning conversations back to their favorite topic. These children are also known to have high intellect and are able to quote facts and details about their topic of interest, often leaving the listener in awe. Many children with Asperger's have echolalia, echoing or repeating phrases heard in movies or other conversations. With much therapy, these kids can learn about social conversation and how to interact with others. Children with Asperger's autism generally have more ability to verbalize and communicate, but they often struggle with social impairments, which they tend not to understand. They crave more peer relationships, yet often they don't grasp what is hindering them from developing such relationships. Asperger's is considered the milder of the two forms of autism, but Asperger's and Kanner's share many of the same symptoms.

Social Problems

Due to the many issues related to autism, children with the disorder often have delayed social development, which can include the inability to relate and interact with other people. Children with autism will have trouble interacting and playing with their own siblings or other children, mainly because they have little or no imaginative play and because they also lack empathy for other people's feelings. At other times, the problem is that their peers simply don't understand them or their autistic behaviors, so they shy away from interacting with them. Some children with autism are more removed and don't really care a great deal about interacting with other kids; others carry deep desires for friendships they don't have.

Obsessions or Obsessive Compulsive Disorder

Nearly all children with autism have areas of obsession or obsessive compulsive disorder (OCD). This can be as mild as always preferring one fast food restaurant or so serious as to devastate the family on a variety of levels. Most parents of a child with autism will tell you that even using a different street to get to a common destination will cause their child to become very unhappy and agitated. Other parents claim their child only has areas of rigidity or "insistence on sameness" regarding clothing brands or other preferences. Children with autism have been said to have photographic memories, often knowing if a parent rearranges decorative items in the house, even in a small way. The rearrangement may be very subtle, but the autistic child knows exactly what has changed. Sometimes, the child will not care about things in one area of the house but be obsessive about things in another area.

For some children, a minor level of OCD can later escalate into a major, life-altering symptom that wreaks havoc on everything and everyone in the household. OCD may present itself early on and then mellow out to something more like a side-symptom that can be worked around. Doctors usually attribute OCD symptoms to the chemical imbalances commonly associated with autism. While children with autism can develop obsessions with just about anything, some of the most common obsessions include televisions shows, videos, books, dinosaurs, Disney movies, trains (Thomas the Tank, a common favorite), planes, electronics, clothing, food, name brands, logos, people, and a preference for one parent all the time. Obsessions can last a very long time, sometimes years before they disappear, often to be replaced by a new one.

Hyperactivity

Hyperactivity, a short attention span, and constant busyness are all symptoms of autism. Many parents and educators have to find ways to gradually lengthen the attention span or find alternate methods to teach the child. Children with autism can't focus nearly as long as a normal child can. They may have a high level of intelligence and absorb a lot of information in the periods of hyperactivity; eventually those who work with them figure this out. Hyperactivity leads to social issues and is a very exhausting part of caring for these children. Hyperactivity also goes hand-in-hand with one of autism's most common symptoms: sleeplessness.

Lack of Natural Fear and Presence of Abnormal Fear

Most children with autism lack natural fear. This is the good fear that is natural in people and helps keep us safe. For this reason, children with autism can have no fear of walking in the street or in a body of water or other potentially dangerous situations. Most children would pause in a state of natural fear when presented with certain scenarios. For example, when approaching the edge of a street of busy traffic, the presence of loud and large vehicles would cause a normal child to pull back. Children with autism must be trained to respond appropriately in such situations. Their parents must verbally and physically train them for those times when natural fear is not present.

By the same token, they can also develop abnormal or unnatural fears to things typical children wouldn't fear at all. Some children with autism fear everyday things, such as stairs, animals, foods, people, and other common things. There is rarely rhyme or reason as to why the child develops such a fear.

Lack of Empathy and Difficulties with Boundaries

Because children with autism lack empathy or the ability to understand life in any way other than what they feel, many of them also have problems understanding boundaries. It is a big accomplishment to get children with autism to understand that some things belong to someone else and that they can't just take anything they see. Lack of empathy and boundary problems are also part of the reason for the social dysfunctions of autism.

Boundaries with food are a common issue for children with autism. Food is seen as something to fix the hunger pang in their own stomachs, and they have been known to grab food off other people's plates when hungry. Food has no specific ownership in the mind of the child; it is seen as merely a cure for what they feel they need. Food in grocery stores is seen in the same light, especially if the child sees something familiar, such as food seen on a TV commercial. These are some of the first social issues parents and teachers must work on to help a child with autism to blend in socially.

Health Problems

Children with autism frequently suffer from chronic health problems, including food and airborne allergies, yeast overgrowth, infections, and gastrointestinal problems. Medical professionals who study autism have found evidence that children with autism have serious immune deficiencies, which are to blame for the host of problems they battle. The lack of immune abilities that help fend off or filter the heavy metals to which children are exposed leaves them vulnerable to heavy metal toxicities; these are among the problems many doctors now treat with natural supplements or nutrient therapy.

Behavior Problems

Children with autism are prone to behavior problems. A great many of these problems are rooted in the various aspects of their autism. For example, if the child cannot talk and has strong obsessions, he or she will get very upset when an item of obsession is gone or doesn't work right. The inability to communicate will frustrate the child, likely leading him or her to throw a tantrum. Sensory problems in and of themselves may cause a child with autism to scream until the situation changes. But children with autism can also develop behavior issues that are just old-fashioned behavior problems. It can be very difficult for parents to discern which problems are related to the autism and which are just the child being a kid. Over time, most parents develop a sense of wisdom and can discern between the two. The greatest problem is that some outsiders think all of the behavior problems are controllable when, in fact, they are not.

What Is an Autistic Savant?

The movie *Rain Man* made the term almost a buzzword for many years. It also caused many people to have the misconception that all people with autism function as highly as the main character in the movie. Autistic savants make up about 10 percent of people with autism. Savants have a level of genius or high intelligence in a specific area, such as math or music. Some can do complex calculations of math in their head almost instantly, while others can recall calendar dates from many years back at a nearly flawless rate. Artistic talents can be an area of giftedness as well. Some savants have musical abilities that suddenly manifest when exposed to a musical instrument, awing those around them with the ability to play the instrument without ever having being taught. Some have perfect pitch and can sing back a tune as if it is a recording of the actual song. Other savants have the ability to glance at a page in a phone book and remember the phone numbers on the page as if they had photographed the page in their memory. It is not unusual for someone with savant abilities to still have trouble overcoming the many other aspects of their autism, such as appropriate behavior in social situations or responding to common dangers in the home.

It is not unusual for children with autism who are not savants to still exhibit giftedness in particular areas that shocks people. Many children will reveal abilities and knowledge that surprise people because nobody ever taught it to them, yet these children already know it. They may not be genius level in their gift, but a very noticeable gift is still present.

What Causes Autism?

This is the million-dollar question to which everyone wants to know the answer. Sometimes genetics is clearly involved in an autism diagnosis, but many other times it is not. Many people believe that there is a link between the preservatives that were once used in vaccines, while others have strong beliefs that the viruses in the vaccinations are the culprit. Many point to airborne or other environmental pollutants as a factor, a theory backed up by studies of cluster cases of autism, cases in which larger percentages of diagnosis exist near towns or cites where certain pollutants are found.

When children with autism are tested, immune deficiencies are commonly found, so the immune system is definitely part of the picture. Some children have seizures or silent seizure activity in the brain, which leads some to believe that this is a causative factor. Parents, doctors, and scientists frequently agree that one thing may set autism in motion, with other factors later compounding it. This explains why treatments are multifaceted and why a variety of approaches is generally necessary for each child. One thing is for sure, there has never been so much work, so many studies, done to discover the causes of autism as there is today. I believe it won't be too many years before the mystery is unraveled. I pray that it helps the next generation.

Interventions and Treatments for Autism

In this section, I give you some of the most popular and most common therapies known in the treatment of autism, but this discussion only brushes the surface of treatments and therapies. Any search of the Internet will provide you with a wealth of knowledge should you decide to read more about autism or any of the treatments I've discussed. See Appendix B for a list of resources.

Natural Therapies and Diets

For years, treatment of autism merely meant what kind of drugs would best calm the child down. And while many people with autism do still take medications and are satisfied with the results, the treatment choices are widening all the time. Many parents now believe their children receive the best level of help by using natural methods supervised by medical doctors who test the body for what is wrong and create a natural treatment plan. These methods are used by more medical clinics than ever before and are highly successful in many cases. Mineral therapy, digestive enzymes, B-vitamin therapies, and substances that fight yeast are just a few of the successful approaches in the natural category of treatment. Restoring gut health is of major importance in the natural treatment of autism.

Special diets are also very beneficial and worth trying, especially if the parents or medical professionals suspect dietary issues. Gluten-free and casein-free diets, as well as the Feingold diet, are among the most popular choices for people with autism. Other diets are often based on specific food allergies. A quick search of the Internet will reveal more treatments for autism, many of them natural.

Anti-fungal and Anti-yeast Treatments

A large percentage of children with autism suffer with yeast infection, also known as Candida overgrowth. This problem is connected to the core problem of immune deficiencies common to children with autism. Prescription drugs can be used to kill the yeast effectively. Some parents find natural supplements to combat the yeast and are very pleased with the results. Probiotics are needed to help restore balance to the gut flora and help prevent yeast overgrowth from occurring again. Yeast overgrowth can flare up any time, and parents must start fighting it all over again.

Occupational Therapy, Speech Therapy, Physical Therapy

Regardless of whether parents use prescription medication or natural approaches to treat their child's autism, most all children with autism receive therapies, especially while they are very young. Occupational therapy is highly beneficial for many of the sensory disturbances that accompany autism. Sensory Integration Therapy is commonly used by occupational therapists to help the child with autism learn to sort out the misfiring of brain signals that produce so many of their sensory disturbances. Sensory Integration Therapy is always finely tuned for each child's individual needs and problems. No two autistic children will have the exact same therapy plans. When successful, it can improve attention, concentration, listening, comprehension, balance, coordination, and impulsivity control.

Speech therapy is a must for children with autism who have speech problems or delays. Speech therapists are always learning new methods in an effort to attain speech victories.

Physical therapy is sometimes needed for people with autism, working together with occupational therapy for a better end result. Sometimes, children receive these therapies at clinics or hospitals; at other times, they are provided in the school environment.

Music Therapy

Music therapy is a method using music to get into the child's world and teach on a different plane, exploiting the rhythm and flow of the music. Music therapists are trained to understand each child differently and create music therapy lessons accordingly. Sometimes the music therapy can be useful in breaking isolation patterns the child with autism may be caught in by providing a relationship of sorts with the music itself. Music therapy is rarely used by itself as the only therapy in a child's treatment; generally, it complements the variety of other therapies the child receives.

Hyperbaric Oxygen Therapy

This is one of the latest in therapies to aid in the treatment of autism. While hyperbaric oxygen therapy has been used for years to assist with the healing of injuries in mainstream society, it has only recently gained the attention of doctors who treat autism. It is increasingly being used to realize benefits in children with autism spectrum disorders because of its ability to deliver greater oxygen levels to the brain and vital organs and to stimulate tissue regeneration. In people with autism, hyperbaric oxygen therapy treatment has been known to improve verbal communication, direct eye contact, reasoning ability, motor skills, balance, and attention span, as well as reducing aggressive behavior.

Applied Behavior Analysis (ABA)

Applied Behavior Analysis is a method of teaching children the skills of normal learning of language, play, and social skills. This method is time intensive and looks very repetitive to the outsider seeing it for the first time. But the instructor is literally training the child's mind to understand how to learn in the real world. Because of the issues the child with autism has to overcome, the how-to is not wired the same way that it is for a normal child. They have to be taught social cues, timing, and exactly what to do and when. In many cases, ABA is taught to the parents, who then implement ABA sessions at home as part of the daily routine. This sounds simplistic to those who first hear about it, but many parents report that it does work and can initiate a turnaround in their child's daily life.

APPENDIX B

Resources

Autism Resources

Autism Research Institute
4182 Adams Avenue
San Diego, CA 92116
866-366-3361
www.autism.com

The Autism Research Institute Web site is filled with valuable information and links you to many other informative Web sites.

Autism Society of America
7910 Woodmont Avenue, Suite 300
Bethesda, MD 20814-3067
800-3AUTISM (800-328-8476)
www.autism-society.org

Autism Society of America offers this marvelous site featuring a wide range of information about autism, including services and online networking. This site is great for anyone, including families of children with autism, wanting to learn more about autism.

Defeat Autism Now!

www.defeatautismnow.com

Defeat Autism Now! is a project of the Autism Research Institute. This site features a wealth of information on autism, including cutting edge treatments and approaches. Of special interest is a physicians directory for anyone seeking to find a DAN! doctor for a child with autism.

National Autism Association

1330 W. Schatz Lane

Nixa, MO 65714

877-NAA-AUTISM (877-622-2884)

www.nationalautismassociation.org

Excellent information about autism is featured on the site of National Autism Association. If you believe you see symptoms of autism in someone you love, this site features a section called "All About Autism" with pages of information and a video to watch showing what autism symptoms look like.

Pfeiffer Treatment Center

4575 Weaver Parkway

Warrenville, IL 60555-4039

866-504-6076

www.hriptc.org

The Pfeiffer Treatment Center is the medical facility spoken of in this book that prescribed nutrient therapies for the autism symptoms of the author's son. They specialize in the treatment of biochemical imbalance, treating patients with symptoms of a wide variety of behavioral disorders.

Ministry & Support Resources

Children of Destiny
PO Box 120607
West Melbourne, FL 32912-0607
www.childrenofdestiny.org
  Children of Destiny is a ministry site built by Jack and Rebecca Sytsema, parents of two children on the autism spectrum. They feature a focus on prayer for autism, both to find the cause and to provide spiritual encouragement to the parents of children with autism. As a free service, they offer an e-mail prayer of the day, written to bless the families of children with autism.

Friendship Ministries USA
2215 29th St SE B6
Grand Rapids, MI 49508
888-866-8966
www.friendship.org
  Friendship Ministries specializes in church programs for the inclusion of all persons with cognitive disabilities. This site includes advice for churches just beginning an inclusion ministry as well as materials specially geared for these programs.

National Challenged Homeschoolers Associated Network
www.nathhan.com / church.htm
  If your church feels led to start an inclusion ministry for children with autism, you may find this site informative. It's another mother's story of autism and will help you understand the necessity of church inclusion for autistic children.

Sibling Support Project
www.siblingsupport.org
  Are you a sibling who needs some support from someone else like yourself? Sibling Support features emotional support for brothers and sisters of anyone with a lifelong disability, including autism.